Writing On

CW01500011

The Poetry Of Tim Noble

edited by **Will Daunt**

with a Preface by **Joanna Clarke**

I
Ormskirk
p
r
i
n
t

Any proceeds from the sale of *Writing On Rock* will be donated to a favourite of Tim's: the Royal Shakespeare Company's Education Department.

The Ormskirk Imprint is a small publishing enterprise based in West Lancashire. It works on a not-for-profit, commission-only basis, with any funds raised from book sales going to a nominated good cause.

For Tim's 'Four Girls'

Joanna, Phoebe, Bryony and Flora

ABOUT THIS BOOK

Researching and compiling this book was like setting out on one of Tim's expeditions: the most invigorating kind of foray into the unknown. It was a project which flourished for having no particular route mapped out from the start. The first rewards were the memoirs and tributes from those who knew Tim. Then a handful of additional poems that he had dedicated to family and friends emerged, alongside three prose pieces. These were joined by poems written by friends and family for the project: all inspired by, or about Tim.

The book reveals Tim's writing in four sections. 'Pastoral Events' explores Tim's life in education, while 'Trawled Deep Into The Heart' features poems about Tim's closer relationships with family and friends. 'Writing On Rock' (the last poetry section) gathers together the work that celebrates Tim's often exhilarating encounters with the natural world. A fourth section includes the prose work

The poetry is by turns lyrical and muscular in tone and personal and universal in the themes that it explores. As an English teacher, Tim knew the rules and the rewards of writing, and as a mountaineer he understood the intricate, intimate nature of the relationship between the climber and the rockface.

In each section's contents page, prose contributions by family, friends and colleagues are in italics.

Tim's work - and poems by other writers - are not.

CONTENTS

For anyone whose life was touched by Tim Noble, the overwhelming memory is a sense of 'bigness'. Bigness in both height and breadth were the obvious and prosaic manifestation of the word (choosing his coffin has to be up there with the saddest and funniest moments of my life); but Tim's bigness was so much more, as those of you will read and to those who have contributed to this collection will know – some of you better than me.

Tim entered my life in 1979 when he 'strutted and fretted' across the stage of our newly formed comprehensive school in rural Bedfordshire. He towered above our puny VIth form frames and most of his colleagues in the staff room, and only the headteacher was louder and scarier. But from the moment I walked into his classroom for my first lesson (*The Merchant of Venice*) my limited and timid 17-year-old mind knew that I had encountered a brain of planetary proportions with a passion to match.

He demanded the most you were able to give and always a little bit more. And once I learned that he applied the same discipline to himself, it was easy to let go of the teenage rebellious indignation and to thrive and grow under his tutelage.

Tim had many passions in his life: mountains, Shakespeare, D.H. Lawrence, Ibsen, Hughes, education in all its forms, his daughters, women and for an all too brief time – me.

We reconnected in 2001, this time as equals and I knew that, for however many years together we were afforded, my life would become a roller coaster of high emotion, huge challenges and deep passion. As a world weary and cynical 40-something I thought I understood Tim's big intellect, his big demands and his big ambitions. I never believed that I could tame them and neither did I want to; but what took me by surprise was the bigness of his heart.

Three and a half years after his death, this bigness continues to surprise me: friends of his who contact me out of the blue tell me about apparently insignificant moments of support, encouragement and love that he showed them, moments that changed their lives for the better; former pupils who e-mail me to recount his interest in and impact on their ambitions; the man in our local corner shop who is keen to share his daughter's exam success because 'Mr. Noble always asked about her and he would have been so pleased'; our neighbour in France who, despite his Auvergnat reserve, wept openly when I told him that the big man in the blue Twingo wasn't coming back.

This poetry collection was in its gestation phases before Tim died. He longed to see his collection in print (not from an inflated sense of ego: he always referred to himself as a modest 'class D' poet, bowing with graciousness to his hero, Ted Hughes) but from a sense of 'not I, not I but the wind that blows through me' – a nod to his other poetic hero, D.H. Lawrence.

As the project was unfinished at the time of his death, I am sure that there is plenty in here that he would have furiously rewritten and edited before it got near the printed page. But in the event, this is not a collection of critically-honed pieces – although I am sure that many of you will find some of them very fine poems indeed. No, this is homage to a man – a man who touched so many lives in so many ways and who gave of himself so freely and without fear or favour.

I don't intend to say too much about the poetry itself. There are better and more objective critics than me who can do this if they wish. I have always believed that poetry speaks to us all in ways that make sense to us as individual readers at any given point in our lives; and that a collective 'informed' response can often be limiting and unhelpful. Suffice it to say that some of the poems are unbearably personal and say so much about my too few and too short years with Tim. Others will resonate with your memories of him and what he meant to you.

I would like to thank those of you who have contributed to the 'birth' of this collection and especially to Will, who has been such a loving and gentle editor at all times. His work has been safe in your hands, Will. Tim knew that it would be.

I would also like to thank those who have helped and supported me on this painful journey glibly referred to as grief – you know who you are.

And lastly I would like to thank Phoebe, Bryony and Flora – our girls. When I used to tease Tim about the dedication he would include in the collection, he would always reply without hesitation – 'my four girls'

So my darlings as we go forward as a brave quartet prepared to face the slings and arrows of outrageous fortune, this is for us: from our Big Man.

Joanna Clarke

Introduction

My last meeting with Tim was accidental. It was May half term, and we bumped into each other in Keswick. Tim had been up to something in the hills – and had come down to buy a painting.

Memory tells me that the purchase was larger than its owner (which was surely impossible) but whether it was or not, we slipped back into the well-worn banter of those days when we'd been colleagues. The routine would invariably involve me asking Tim whether he really thought something was a good idea. In turn, Tim would resolve that if the idea hadn't been a good one, it surely was (now that I'd suggested that it wasn't).

There were many joys of working with Tim in the English Department of the only comprehensive school in Salisbury. It was the second half of the 1980s, and we flourished upon the kind of professional freedoms that made us consider carefully what and how we taught: the team ethic was everything. To the outsider it probably made many English Departments seem formidable (or perhaps *we* thought we were formidable, and everyone else simply had us down as bloody-minded).

Tim was a great standard bearer for our cause: larger and louder than life, and more than ready to go over the top and do battle with senior staff, other departments, parents and anyone else who was compromising our deeper (and sometime rather esoteric) purposes. Obviously, we would always try to check that he had the right gear in his kitbag, and we loved to hear how the latest skirmish had turned out. In the unlikely event that any of Tim's courageous forays hadn't quite gone to plan, he would laugh at himself with that infectious, boyish giggle.

His love of climbing, drama and Shakespeare coloured much of his work, and (in the best possible sense) we never quite knew what was coming next. Whether it was school shows, or the arrival of authors who climbed (or climbers who wrote), Tim's vision enlivened the place. He even managed to persuade me to appear as an ancient peasant in a production of *Lark Rise To Candleford*, the sight and sound of which traumatized my wife for years afterwards.

About five years ago, Tim phoned me and began to describe the poems that he had been writing for a long time. They weren't something that we'd discussed before, but I wasn't surprised: he'd been supportive of my various scribbling, always.

With particular diffidence, Tim asked if there was any way that I'd be prepared to help him shape the work into a collection, and I said that I would be pleased to do so. Very sadly, we did not speak again, and this wasn't just because of the large distance between Leigh-on-Sea and Lancashire. The project was particularly dear to Tim, and I can imagine him thinking that he couldn't possibly "send it up to Will" until it was "really ready".

Of course, I now wish that I'd phoned him to suggest that such things are never finished, but, in the event, when Joanna sent me the manuscript, I knew that we had something substantial: not quite complete, but as large and rewarding in its scope as the man himself was.

Most poignant was the list of poems, in Tim's hand. It was dated, 'Oct. 2014': in other words, only weeks before he left us. 36 poems are named, nearly all of which are included here. Tim asterisked three and Joanna tells me that 'At Takstang Monastery' and 'The Graves of the Poets' were never written. However, she described to me the setting of the latter poem, and I have written a piece with the same title. Just before publication, Tim's account of that trip was discovered and, it is included here, with two other pieces of prose.

The collection's working title was 'Pastoral Events', which I decided to transfer to a sub-section. *Writing On Rock* was more powerful and evocative: a statement about the core of the poetry, and the process of Tim's writing.

Would Tim have approved of this presumptuous reshuffle? I hope so. Perhaps I have some previous experience of not quite doing what Nobility required of me, and of getting away with it – and of Tim's forgiving smile. Who knows ..?

My insubordination – if that's what it was – went further and I divided the project into three parts. This wasn't difficult, because most of the poems fell happily into one of the following areas: work, family and friends or climbing.

But the collection needed a distinctive structure most because of its other defining feature: the writing *about* Tim. Inviting colleagues, fellow climbers and family to respond to Tim's work was something that Joanna and I agreed to do early on. The poems and the man are so full of life that they demand a bigger project than simply the familiar 'slim volume' of verse that they might have been, otherwise.

Joanna's input was invaluable here: I know no more about climbing than how to reach the thirteenth stair in our house, and, at the outset, I had met none of the book's potential contributors. She threw out the net, and hauled in a very fine catch of those who wanted to say something about Tim and/ or his poetry. We avoided a proscriptive brief and encouraged people to write as little or as much of what they wanted to, in response to some of the poems.

There was an impressive and stirring response, the pieces varying in style and length. Many thanks to all. The subject matter ranges from brother Jeremy's piece about childhood to poignant and evocative reflections on family and school life and, of course, expeditions and climbs. Several contributors have written their own poems, including Tim's daughter, Br.

Then another poem of Tim's - 'Epithalamium'- emerged, thanks to Richard Brown, who explains its genesis later on. By chance, it's near the centre of the book, underlining the particular gift Tim had for deploying landscape to determine the nature of love:

> But for *this* husband and *this* wife,
> filled chambers of their heart will be

tied always to the flashing cliffs,
above the caverns of the sea.

In each of the book's three sections of poems, Tim's work speaks first, without interruption. Reflections follow, encouraging the reader to enjoy the poems exactly as they are, before taking in the bigger picture, In this way the fifteen or so responses to Tim's work enhance without ever being in danger of "taking over".

A similar approach is adopted in the fourth part of the book, which features Tim's prose writing.

The first section of the book retains that 'Pastoral Events' designation. These six poems are rooted in Tim's experience of teaching and are pastoral in at least two ways. First we feel – and sometimes see – the countryside from the classroom window, something that was certainly possible from our English department, at the western-most edge of Salisbury. A poem like 'Pastoral Events' itself is a carefully wrought study of the rigours of upland sheep farming and that other kind of *pastoral*: the work of the teacher:

If sheep founder in cold winds, more than lambs are lost.

It's the same at school. I shepherd all my flock out
in the gale swept playgrounds of their youth.

In 'Lydiard Park', the natural world is once again knocking, as it were, at the classroom door, inspiring and distracting equally, but 'Artist' (in its tribute to Roland Hilder) reconstructs one of the early influences on Tim's writing. The poem makes vivid the impact of the painter's art on the young writer's imagination. Hilder and Tim's work have some common characteristics: conciseness, the creation of a sense of place and the honed and original depiction of the natural world.

The book's longest section is also its most intimate: hence its title, 'Trawled Deep Into The Heart'. At the core of these powerful poems are eight sonnets, which I have grouped as a sequence. This does not appear to have been Tim's original plan, but his accomplished use of the form drew them together in the editing process. They have a common and compelling language that shapes the love of friend and family with the patience and skill of an artisan.

'At Sea Palling' is a similarly elemental poem about Tim's childhood: the adult remembering two boys' sense of wonder as their father (Tim's Dad) set about leading the repair of a critical section of the Norfolk sea wall.

Four further poems only existed in Tim's list of contents and in personal copies, given to Joanna. They show a very different side to the writer, eschewing the hewn and large-scale vision of many of Tim's 'outdoor' poems.

For example, 'My Sweet Woman' and 'My Sweet Man' mirror each other's intimate yet humorous language. At the same time, their shared construction is less formal and more speculative. Another, 'Dependency' challenges the reader with the swell and decline of its shape, and the inversion of gender. Conversely, 'Your Trees' is poignantly simple.

The section is humorous and self-deprecating in places. The ironical word games of 'The Riddle Of Love' sit comfortably alongside the grotesque absurdities recreated in 'Pig': the portrayal of a ghastly moment in Carcassone.

The mountains and the draw of the great outdoors are reserved for the third section, which includes two photographs we found in Tim's manuscript. My walks with Tim rarely extended further than the staff room, but I was a bystander during the gestation and birth pangs of his epic *Great VS Climbs in the Lake District*, published by David and Charles in 1989. As colleagues, we always knew when Tim was "up to something" and at breaks and during other spare moments, he could be found pawing at his tiny portable typewriter, like a bear trying to scrape the last drops of honey from the pot.

That was, of course an undigitized and more innocent age, and it's remarkable that Tim could produce such a fine book, while running a large English department and raising a young family. If you don't own a copy, try to pick one up online. It's worth having for the photographs alone – often of tiny figures suspended against spectacular rock faces: specks of radiant gear on vast escarpments. You'll pick out Tim and many of his climbing colleagues – including some who've contributed to this venture.

At the heart of the 'Writing On Rock' section lie poems that capture – even tame, briefly – the untold forces of the natural world. There's the prehistoric 'Stone Bull' painted and imprisoned on rock by another artist, or the ship's boiler in the title poem, a tiny manmade marker for climbers, adrift in a sea of stone.

The camaraderie of climbing – friendships linked by the real and metaphorical ropes of the mountains – is the backbone to many of these poems. In 'Climber' and the terrifying 'Bow Wall' the interdependency of each team member is acutely shown; other pieces, like 'Dharlang Valley Expedition, 1979' and 'A View To Kanjiroba' set this sense of common enterprise against bewitching backdrops.

As the book was nearing completion, Joanna sent me a series of photographs of the only copy of 'Where Men And Moorland Meet', written for *The Dalesman* in the late 1980s. The story is a revelation, pinpointing and reviving a powerful moment in a particular corner of the western Dales. The narrator is as good as Tim as we might want them to be, and the hostile late winter landscape is sculpted in our imaginations with extraordinary skill. Here, a dutiful and admiring apprentice pays tribute to the craft and tenacity of the hill farmer – qualities that characterized Tim's own climbing and writing. And the story is told, a story that Tim had perhaps also intended to versify, since the title is included in his original list of poems.

Mentioned earlier, the journalistic piece, 'The Graves Of The Poets' emerged with a third gem, near the time of going to press. Written in 1986, 'Two Falls and Two Submissions', is an exhilarating and yet playful account of a hairy climb up Ben Nevis.

There is great poetry in the language of each of these very different prose pieces, explaining further why they had to be included here.

And as well as "To Rest Is Not To Conquer", there is a lot more to the whole collection. Poems like 'Your Trees', 'Silbury Hill' and 'A Wave Of The Sea' have a particular lyrical charm. There is ingenious use of traditional forms in 'Villanelle' and the 'Dharlang Valley' sonnet. Like 'Dependency' and 'The Riddle Of Love', 'Rain Forest' shows Tim experimenting with form and subject matter, choosing judiciously when to exploit and when to avoid the taut rhythms and evocative diction that run through 'Tuolomne Meadows, California'. Like 'Sailing To Africa', that poem unravels the tensions of relationships through uncompromising and provocative imagery. We're thrown into:

> …Indian country …
>   …where the stone of moonlight
> hones Tressider Peak - not yet buried
>
> in a scalp of stars and Glacier Lake,
> by day a clear trinket, mirror-tracks
> an old canoe's thin dribble of wake.

Tim's preliminary contents page suggests that these thirty or so poems were the first chapter of a larger project. He wanted to shape and formulate them into a finished piece. That has been done. What else he might have written, what else he dreamt of, can be constructed by our imaginations and memories. But the reflections about the writer that are included here take us further on that sometimes painful, often enriching journey, rediscovering the good and understanding the legacy of a man of the mountains, a mountain of a man.

Tim's still with us, in the poems and the wider writing. Share them.

Will Daunt

PASTORAL EVENTS

Pastoral Events

Twenty years ago, April gales buffeted moors
above my school and steel clouds scoured the dish of land
clean of colour. Shrapnel wind bursts snapped classroom doors shut
on slow fingers; tore marking out of closed hands;

pounded us into a soft concussion of fatigue.
I taught, but thought of sheep field-bound above the farm,
bulldozed by the blasts. With wind and gritstone in league
to make shelter round the compass a rage of calm,

ewes were giving birth straight into the tearing sheets
of polar air. I swapped red pen for crook and knife
at dusk, roamed battered fields to listen for the bleats
of broken, frozen lambs. In some we found, the life

had gone too soon, stamped out by a mother whose
milk was leaking freely down the wind. Then our knives
flashed in torchlight; we'd strip a fleece from legs and hooves
still warm and womb-soft on the bitter grass. The live

sheep worry-nuzzled at the bag of skin and bones,
puzzled by a mute, accusing sky-stare of ox-
like eyes, already cold-glazing. On icy stones
by our barn I'd sling the carcass, away from fox

and crows, dress an orphan lamb in the bloody, knotted coat,
then brusquely urge this shocked survivor to court
a life from the proud, bewildered killer's clotted
teats. I was a shepherd caring for a flock, taught

by my farmer-landlord how to feel, look and act.
There was nothing in books at school to help me sort
the problems of those lambasted fields, just the facts
of death or life, of nature red in hoof and claw.

Though that was in another time and place, the wind
this April is the same, finds me study-bound, more
than lamb-life or words of texts weighing on my mind.
Now I care for another flock for whom the laws

of nature mean about as much as ancient games
on their computers. But the past returns: nurture
of all young lambs is still my main concern. Names
of children who sob themselves into a rapture

14

of distress because they miss their mother I can
rehearse word perfect, like those fields above the farm.
And the others: lost along the path from boy to man,
who look at me as if I want to do them harm.

There's one here now, outside the door. Sam's expecting
punishment, fine-honed anger at the very least.
Inside, looking anywhere but me, rejecting speech,
he stands aloof, a skeleton at the feast

of life in school. Bruised by the simple fact that other
children have a beauty that he doesn't want to own
he has in himself as well, he blames his mother,
father, brothers, me, the school for making him alone.

The economies of upland farms hang on threads
of wool. When storms blow arctic through the spring and frost
blights new grass, how will farmers earn their daily bread?
If sheep founder in cold winds, more than lambs are lost.

It's the same at school. I shepherd all my flock out
in the gale swept playgrounds of their youth: boys like Sam
and girls who loathe their dads. But every year brings doubts:
for how can shepherds fear the violence of the lambs?

Lydiard Park

'Learn of the green world what can be thy place.' Ezra Pound, Cantos 81

From my classroom I can see
how the school ends suddenly
at a fence, where eighty trees,
prefect-still, watch jealously
over pockets of hot shadow.

This is an edge of order:
released, pupils run the baize
playing field to its border
with domestic turf; then laze,
flirt, shout and rest, furiously.

Two boys, keen to share the guilt
of a smut of smoke, crash past
a rash of nettles wilting
by the stile, into the vast
secret garden of the park.

Lydiard is landscaped in light.
Here, all natural things need names
drawn from art, because they're right,
like a painting of a game:
that flight of birds becomes a spurt;

a surgeon up a tree lops
limbs in a theatre of air.
The boys are lost for words, stop
blurting smoke and gossip, stare
into the maze of distance.

There are lessons to be learned,
but back in school: how the green
world has its place; why words earned
there help us make our meanings,
and when to ask the questions.

Artist

(for Roland Hilder)

Kind aunts sent me your paintings
reproduced on Christmas cards.
The wall above my bed became a
gallery; the drawer below, a catalogue.

I tried to paint like you - came first
in Art ("hardly a subject") at thirteen.
But this was for a study of light on
house roofs, not a studied landscape.

Practising to hold a brush and load
it with the muted colours, forms
and subjects of the Home Counties
(where I knew you must have lived),

I mastered only hybrids such as
'Dutch Barn Brown', 'Winter Grey'.
Beyond these though, was your skill
and Art, which I could never grasp.

For in your eye's frame, faint smells of
winter wood keep late swallows
in perpetual motion. In outland
comers of the canvas, light-frightened

hedgehogs lie curled round dreams
of grubs and midnight saucers of
moon. On a smooth hill, a cottage
smokes, its roots far underground,

stitching the anarchy of earth to
an ordered tonal patchwork quilt
of fields, while washed by pale sun,
the land steadies after a stumble into rain.

Under your brush, there is always
some rook-roosting, furrow-fathering
tree, scratching on the sightless
sky in the perfect braille of the wind.

Shaw Farm Vice

At midday the barn begins to tick
like a bomb. Roof metal, braced against
the heat, puckers, corrugates, mutters
rust flakes as it warms. Moving into
the darkened novelty of coolness,
I side-step shadow bars and explore
this deep hangar space.

To be surprised: sunbeams, stronger than
steel struts shore up cracked glass. The air is
solid, heavy, stale, warmer than a
greenhouse can effect. To the dim barn
end, piles of domestic junk are laid
out carefully in tythes with aisles: here's
paradise reclaimed.

Each pile could be contents of a home:
old hoovers nozzle up against one
another to dribble tales of dust;
mangled washing machines ooze oil
from rusted drums; pigeon shit laces
a wrecked armchair to make a stinking
antimacassar.

Nothing is missing or mislaid, each
heap graded for size, shape, genus.
Five doors, face to face in three square feet,
open onto nothing but themselves;
three rank mattresses, indented, lie
side by side in sin, a trunk spills soiled
sheets, indiscretely.

All of this is going nowhere else,
surely? I think of likely owners:
young professionals in smart red homes
around the farm, keen to live off pine,
stainless steel and credit. What does 'New'
mean to likely buyers: the poor,
the homeless, dispossessed?

Bemused in the lanes of cool concrete,
I almost miss the workbench set in door-spilled
light and an iron vice, man-heavy,
bulldog-clamped around a child's balloon.
Helpless in the force-field of this joke,
I poke in dusty wood shavings for
reasons or a sign.

Teachers are 'Learning about Learning'
with me at Shaw Ridge Farm; the morning
task: chart in words or paint "change of state".
Surrounded by life's detritus, I
wait now for the child-like carpenter
who will help me change and take the vice
from the green balloon.

Villanelle

Each season, Summer, Winter, Spring, I see
primary pupils. "Will you," teachers say,
"suffer little children who come to me

not knowing how to understand, or be
themselves?" "Yes," I reply, "they'll grow and play;
each season, Summer, Winter, Spring, I see

them older, stronger, yearning to be free
of childhood. My colleagues change, too, as they
suffer little children who come. To me,

this growth and change through learning's like a tree
in Eden: blooms and ripened fruits are laid
each season. Summer, Winter, Spring, I see

new pupils' parents regularly. We
agree: in trouble, both school and child may
suffer. Little children who come to me

soon learn the adult world's inconstancy;
so pity some lost leavers who, each day
each season, Summer, Winter, Spring, I see
suffer. Little children! Who come to me?"

Teaching Shakespeare

The boy in front of me fish-grins,
impudently, knowing it's a sin
to flick rolled snot two tables back
at his friends. They've just sealed a pact
to resist the morning's lesson.

For some, this enforced silence
of the pens is prison sentence:
their reprieve, a mate's biro squeak.
Some would give anything to speak
of nothing. Embarrassed by thought,

they shuffle paper, books and shoes
for reassurance, fear to lose
themselves in the dense maze of text.
I look daggers; but soon, the next
minute arrives, needs defining

by sound. I know all their writing
- words and style and hand: exciting
moments are often lurid set
pieces from films that someone's let
them see. They love murder stories.

The girls are tense, witchflick hair whips;
gaze at red-painted fingers; grip,
as they read the Queen's impassioned
words, their imagined babies, dashed
just now against the wall. The boys

preen: pens down, they're warrior-caste.
"Who cares where the heir's gone?" "The last
king was a wimp." "Soft, he deserved
to die." I demur; say, "Reserve
your judgment; see what 'brave' Macbeth

becomes." Then turning to the rest:
"Just think of Brady, Hindley, West
and, 'There's no art to find the mind's
construction in the face'. Don't blind
yourself to the fact of evil."

The lesson ends ambiguously:
life shocks more than art (seriously),
but the boy in front takes the play
home and doesn't grin. I dare say
he's now somewhere he has never been.

Shaw Farm Vice

I didn't attend the particular "Learning about Learning" course to which Tim refers in 'Shaw Farm Vice', but I did attend others. Shaw Ridge is a part of the Western Expansion of Swindon, where Tim taught as a senior teacher at Greendown Community School*. The expansion took place on old farm land and the Shaw Ridge Farm to which Tim refers became an education centre.

The Learning about Learning Project was led by the then English Adviser for Wiltshire, Pat D'Arcy, an inspirational leader with whom Tim had a strong bond. She, like Tim, was very interested in the process by which we learn and in helping others to learn more about the art of teaching creatively. Pat set up a series of residential courses for teachers called Learning about Learning, which ran for the first week of the summer holidays. They were open to all teachers, both primary and secondary and were quite a commitment at the end of the long summer term. Course members each led a session based on one of their favourite lessons. The rest acted as the class, and afterwards reflected individually on what aspects of the lesson had helped or hindered their learning. The sessions could range from finger painting led by a reception class teacher to one on Shakespearean sonnets by a secondary English teacher such as Tim. As you can imagine, this could be stressful for the presenting teacher and those trying to respond intelligently to the sonnets, but they were not so for someone as confident as Tim.

I remember a weekend post-course gathering when Pat brought along a friend of hers, James Britton, who had written a seminal work called Language and Learning. There was an intense discussion between James and Tim on a somewhat esoteric aspect of language, which the rest of us agreed was well above our intellectual level! We were glad Tim was there to keep the side up. He was a powerful intellectual force.

Richard Brown

* Greendown bordered Lydiard Park, and is now Lydiard Park Academy

Teaching Shakespeare

Tim loved teaching Shakespeare to children. Part of his role at Greendown School in Swindon was primary/secondary liaison between it and its feeder schools. Tim (with typical confidence not initially completely shared by the schools involved) chose Shakespeare as the vehicle for building links and set about convincing each school that they could, with his support, put on a Shakespeare play.

Tim often visited the primary school in Trowbridge where I was headteacher and such was my confidence in him that when he suggested that we also put on a Shakespeare play I jumped at the opportunity. We chose *The Tempest* and Tim set about convincing us that all 230 children, aged 4-11 could take part. And that's what happened.

The key to success was Tim's approach. He insisted that all of the older children had a copy of the play and that every word that was spoken was as Shakespeare had written it. He paired some older and younger classes and the youngest children learned their lines as group renditions. Each pair of classes was given a scene from which to capture the essence of the story by selecting the essential lines and to develop action to go with them as groups or individuals as appropriate. Tim believed that children would love the rhythm and sound of Shakespeare's words and would learn them easily, unworried by their strangeness. He was right.

Several weeks of hard work resulted in the most memorable event of my teaching career and experiences that I'm sure many of the children will never forget.

Richard Brown

The Perfect Braille of the Wind

I met Tim in September 1968 at Kingston upon Hull College of Education. We found ourselves on the same course studying English and Drama and Telecommunication. These days I suppose the latter would be dubbed Media Studies. We spent up to ten hours together each week in lectures over a three year period. During that time we got to know each other well and struck up a firm friendship which lasted 46 years.

That itself is interesting because we came from what you might call different sides of the track. Me, scruffy, arrogant grammar school boy, council house, first generation higher education. He was the opposite, well turned out, sure of himself, privileged from generations of success and affluence. Or so it seemed.

In reality we agreed that we were both scared little boys chasing little girls who were frightened to death of us little boys but didn't show it. Retrospection is a great thing isn't it? If only we had known then what we knew now. Tim always that he said looked back on our Hull days with affection. Ah well.....

We were both rebels and the 1960's were a time of rebellion, *pas de rigueur*.

At the end of the three years we went our separate ways and drifted off to teach in different places. There were no addresses to exchange because we didn't know where we were doing or what we would get ourselves into.

It wasn't until the 1970's that we met up again and like most genuine friendships we picked up things from where we had left off. By now we were both Heads of English Departments. Tim was involved in running the Ilkley Literature Festival too. I had travelled to see Ted Hughes. Tim had always been a passionate Hughes "fanatic". Hughes read the whole of 'Crow' that night in a very dramatic and sinister manner.

From then on we did keep in touch. In the 80's Tim was editing the Journal of the National Association of English Teachers. I sent a copy of a text book I had published for him to review. He was very gracious in his comments. Tim was, in fact, gracious in everything he did.

Later in the 90's we had both reached the dizzy heights of senior leadership in schools. We were also going through some interesting times in our own personal lives. I would describe this period of my life, using Mr Dylan words' as "another lifetime full of toil and blood." Tim would more readily turn to Mr. Shakespeare's "slings and arrows of outrageous fortune". You didn't have to be in Tim's company long before you became aware of his passion for Shakespeare.

Phone calls, post cards and Christmas cards came and went between us. By now Tim had left teaching and started his Shakespeare Company for Schools in conjunction with Oxford Brookes University.

Tim was magnificent and although charisma is certainly an overused and little understood word, Tim certainly had charisma. He could shine out and delight company wherever he was. I was always in awe of Tim. We will have to travel a long way in the universe to anything that is superior to human beings at their best. Tim was such a human being.

When we had got to our time of life, he and I, we both recognised that we were only passing through and like so many others. I miss him. I miss him a great deal.

Looking at the section of his poetry collection called 'Pastoral Events', a title which readily recalls his time in education, his time teaching, what might we discover? As I have already said we trained to teach together, often questioning what we were taught about how to teach, how learners learn and what is on offer to be learnt. There were no satisfactory answers then and indeed there seem to be none now, in an educational world of school league tables which operate in the strait jacket of examinations which in turn determine teachers' pay. Rather amusingly or not so really, quite the opposite, one of the facts we learnt about the evolution of schools and education on our course was there was something called Payment by Results in Victorian schools where teachers were paid by children's retention of facts. In Dickens' Hard Times Mr. Gradgrind the teacher says;

> "Now, what I want is, Facts. Teach these boys and girls nothing but Facts. Facts alone are wanted in life. Plant nothing else, and root out everything else. You can only form the minds of reasoning animals upon Facts: nothing else will ever be of any service to them."

Very little seems to have changed. Tim's writing about schools and education reflects this and much more. He is writing in a tradition that echoes for example, D.H. Lawrence's observations from a teacher's point of view in the poem 'Last Lesson of the Afternoon'. Similarly, Barry Hines offers in A Kestrel for a Knave what Hines himself called his "little book about education" - a vision of the brutality and utter futility of a system that does not allow Billy Casper chance or opportunity. Willy Russell's Our Day Out tackles the challenges head on in a manner which brings laughter and tears in equal proportion. It is of course interesting to see that lack of progress for working class boys - particularly in the north of England - is still a major cause of concern. So what we are seeing in Tim's poetry is a confirmation of these ideas and much more.

In 'Pastoral Events' we find a poem which uses the extended metaphor of pastoral care, a phrase much in vogue in the 1960's which has continued in educational circles in the belief that offering this kind of care can help students overcome their own difficulties . Pastoral care is intended to embrace the needs of young people over and above whatever is taught in lessons and indeed return them to classroom and encourage them to make progress according to targets, so that the school does well in the eyes of OFSTED and scores highly in league table positions. A rather cynical view I know but like Tim I have spent some forty years in education. Of course, some pastoral care is magnificent but then again some is disturbing in its lack of emotional intelligence. Of that I am sure Tim would agree.

Another major theme is the restriction of the system, clearly intellectually but also geographically. Tim is all too aware of how schools are shut off from reality. In 'Lydiard Park' the teacher (I think it is always safe to assume that Tim is the teacher in all the poems about school) says:

> From my classroom I can see
> how the school ends suddenly
> at a fence.

In the poem boys released from school run off into "The secret garden of the park" and find they can "Flirt, shout and rest, furiously". They can share "the guilt of a smut of smoke". They can share the dangerous world outside the classroom, take risks and grow.

The last but one poem in this section, 'Teaching Shakespeare' may offer the answer to some of the questions Tim asks in his work. How should we encourage pupils to learn and what to learn? How do teachers teach and what do they teach? It is fitting that this poem is the last poem. We could suggest that everything in this section and indeed in Tim's teaching career has been building towards what happens next.

Leonard Cohen wrote "there is a crack in everything, where the light gets in". Tim was all too well aware of the cracks in the educational system and saw a chance to let the light in. Frustrated by the formality and restrictions of schools and the educational system itself, as echoed in the poems in this section, he saw a way in which he felt he could attempt to offer solutions to some of these problems.

Tim left teaching and established a theatre company under the auspices of Oxford Brookes University. This company took Shakespeare into schools, not to help students understand Shakespeare and to help them pass exams (as so often is the case) but to allow them to understand Shakespeare for its own sake. He believed that the plays were universal in what they had to say about the human condition, both then and now. And of course this was most immediate when the plays were brought to life not by offering a performance in the school hall but by using the text and situations in classrooms and encouraging and allowing pupils to act them out with the help of actor teachers.

Clearly to attempt to do this would difficult. Real education is never easy. If it was there would be no problems. We see this in the poem which echoes other poems in this section.

From the beginning we are aware that the pupils are school refusniks.

> They have just sealed a pact
> To resist the morning's lesson
>
> For some this enforced silence

Of pens is prison sentence.

Then the change comes. The light gets in. The teacher realises that they all love murder stories. *Macbeth* fits the bill.

The girls are tense, witchflick hair whips
Gaze at red-painted fingers; grip,
As they read the Queen's impassioned
Words, their imagined babies, dashed
Just now against the world.

The boys react in similar fashion, seeing themselves as Macbeth. Suspension of disbelief fades until someone realises that monsters like this still exist in the form of the Bradys et al. So this stuff does connect with a reality the students know and gives them plenty to ponder.

The lesson ends ambiguously as the best lessons often do. And the point of the poem follows: indeed what we might see as the point of not only the poem but education itself. As with so many poets the last line confirms the meaning. So here we have the point revealed in the last line, not only of this poem but also the last line of the whole section. This is what we have been leading to.

One boy is now "Somewhere he has never been."

This is where Tim wants Shakespeare to take the boy - to help him understand some of what he has experienced, help him ask questions. But most importantly at this time leave him in this somewhere to wonder and ponder before he returns perhaps having seen something in the maze of distance that may help him to take some small steps forward in his own growth.

I now want turn to the poem 'Artist'. It is dedicated to Roland Hilder. Rowland Hilder (1905–1993)was an English marine and landscape artist and book illustrator. His interest in the countryside (initially of Kent) began a lifelong passion for drawing landscapes in both pencil and watercolour, "The Garden of England", and the Thames with its sailing vessels. Tim admires Hilder's work, and he had been good at Art at school. In fact, he tells us he "came first in Art". The phrase counterbalances somewhat cynically with "hardly a subject" - no doubt a comment from a teacher that only reflects and amplifies a repetitive theme close to Tim's heart.

We find time and time again in his work, that teachers and schools do not really value what may be necessary for real spiritual growth. It might be worth reminding ourselves that Tim is clearly not alone in championing this cause. John Berger says in his *Success and Failure of Picasso* "that to find delight in culture may well be the highest form of human happiness."

Yet Tim does suggest that he was not "really good at Art" in the way Hilder or any painter was. Tim goes on to say merely he himself had the ability to copy. Interestingly enough, insecurity with regard to apparent skills was something that Tim never seemed to reveal but then again surely few of us if any are beyond self-doubt.

However the second half of the poem confirms without any doubt whatsoever Tim's magnificent ability with words. In the last four stanzas he shows a skill that few have. He describes Hilder's paintings in such a detailed and beautiful manner that we can see them in our minds' eye. He turns sublime pictures into glorious poetry.

> In outland
> corners of the canvas, light frightened
>
> hedgehogs lie curled round dreams
> of grubs and midnight saucers of
> moon.

Again in the last stanza the full impact of the poem tells us;

> Under your brush, there is always
> some rook-roosting, furrow fathering
> tree, scratching on the sightless
> sky in the perfect braille of the wind.

We feel the "braille" of that wind as we read because we cannot see the painting itself by the very nature of what is happening. We only have Tim to rely on in being able to complete the task that he has set himself, that is passing on to the reader in words the power of the painting. There can be little doubt that his success is sublime.

Bill Allison

At Sea Palling

At Sea Palling, the sea's a land
swallower; takes choppy moon
bites out of eastern England;
wills down the crumbs of coast
with draughts of bitter waves.

Small and serious we played
hide and seek there in spiky grass,
on the dusty strand; saved
all Norfolk a hundred times
from famine, fear and flood

with Dinky excavators, spades
and trucks. We built strong dykes in
dunes until boys and toy blades
were clogged with grit. Bundled
home to wash away the noise

of air, sea and machines; then filled
with tea, toast and buns, we lay
awake, ear to ear, quiet and still,
while warring warriors of waves
fought all night for our caravan.

From Kings Lynn to Lowestoft,
a berserk invasion from the north
whips white horses to the soft
cliffs each year; in 'fifty three, made sea
fields above the bleak contour of surf.

So, at Sea Palling, father built steel
groynes to slow the long-shore drift.
They're still there now, like keels
of raiding boats with rusty strakes:
boys' nightmares in the barrow dunes.

Perhaps we thought he'd stand
as in the photo: always Canute-like,
engineer against the enemies of tides.
But now, half-concealed, feet on shifting sand,
each day's a nightmare from which he seeks to hide.

My Sweet Woman	My Sweet Man

writes considered rounded	types on his keyboard
long hand	one-fingered
collects moonlight	collects sunlight
in her glass of white wine	in his glass of red wine
swears frequently at drivers	makes raindrops
who upset her equilibrium	on his car windscreen
when she is talking on the phone	slalom through the white lines
on a hard road soft with love	in the middle of the road
and tired of driving	when he's bored with driving
says she loves me from a distance	says he loves me from a distance
in the middle of meetings	between the covers of a novel
I have told her to subvert	I have told him to read

Pig

Carcassone, September 2012

The flying pig came as a big shock:
splayed and squealing, it fell past
a hundred feet of castle rock.
Grounding over mailed heads, its last
meal spilled; became a carcass from a Carcas.
Behind battlements, the dame grinned;
all would be saved; bells sounded.
What the pig had eaten sent besiegers
home crying: the city let them pass.
On the path below the wall
we were disbelievers, too; but later,
crying, splayed and squealing,
we held tight to our pig, saved its bacon.

Dependency

Promise
by love
you offer me
to quit your (in)dependency.
No more fruit of vine
shall fuel your sad, proud despondency –
unless you drink in and of mine
eyes from that deep well I let only
you (of all men see). Be drunk on me,
love, or never more taste grape. You are my Anthony;
I, your unchanged Cleopatra. In our new-found Alexandria,
my chilled fingers will tremble when I see
how flushed by love, not wine, your
dear face can be. True intoxication's
true dependency: you and me.
So live long, love -
to live that
life with
me

EIGHT SONNETS

1. Silk Road

Not through my lens, but by some other eyes
you're framed. From that stupendous view they choose
to snap just you, the camera never lies.
Tibetan refugees think it's a ruse
that Chinese camel drivers have contrived·
to release the shutter on your quick smile
before they're pictured or the sky's arrived.
Beside you, all seek space to rest awhile,
get settled, be themselves. Though desert dust's
a film, this bright transparency's what's best:
back-lit, sharply-focused, eyes wide with trust.
I've a camera; I know what's true. So, lest
others take photos and their hearts to you,
show me your heart, and a framed picture, too.

2. Silk Road

Poring over the silk route map, I know
little of the rich places but the names
we read about and where I want to go.
Following a guide's a rough and tumble game
- especially in the dark: it's all been seen
by others in the past and nothing's new.
But maps can show that 'here' may also mean
the same as 'there' and between the two, few
delights I fear, or ways of turning back
And what if we lose love's bearings now? Which
way to turn; whose baggage gets unpacked?
Dearly, steppes to the east won't make us rich,
so, since I am encompassed in your lap,
you be our guide and compass, read my map.

3. Bryony

Day-long my daughter has defied the sea:
breasting the big waves; racing rollers home
to Crawford Tartan and a flask of tea.
Sand has been her playmate. Alone, she's roamed
the known horizon: cool pools to hot dunes;
skipping across her tracks, a brazen beach
girl, followed heel on heel by pleasure runes.
At four, half-seen through sand-steam (beyond reach),
she taught me how to surf late fatherhood.
At eight - fed, tented and down-deep in sleep -
her salted hands reached out, clasped mine (that should
have held her over every wave). But steep
tsunami of dream took them, then, to seize
her found necklace - a little piece of sea.

4. For Paul Chidgey

Everything I learned about you I found
curled inside Andy's hand at your funeral.
You were a passer by nature; loved sounds
of foot, bat and racket on leather. A ball
well thrown, well caught, could move you more than looks:
nothing else much mattered. A team of friends
and family, churning sand into the book
of effort was a core belief - might mend
the world's worst. You cared for trajectory:
the perfect pitch's parabola of flight.
So, brought to the moment of your story's
ending, how did you know that ball you'd smite,
set bouncing, arcing almost out of view,
we'd catch forever; hold out just for you.

5. Phoebe

Aged four, I thought you'd never jump or skip
or hop: on knees I bounced red balls to you,
inflated world-big, so you would not trip
into fear of fall or failure. I threw
so many things, I nearly lost your youth.
It took the dolls lined up, a whiteboard, books
and dressing up to find a teaching truth:
the world inside your head was huge and looked
just like those balls you'd learned to catch. I found
I could not 'jump the life to come'; moved east.
You trawled deep into the heart; knuckled down;
taught yourself to claim a seat at life's feast.
So, when they told you what you now could seize,
you jumped and skipped, but I was on my knees.

6. Time

Time was when we made time for Time:
untouched by watch hands or a true clock's face,
we didn't find that 'bank where the wild thyme
grows', nor ride to win 'Time's winged chariot' race
(or from Time's bank we might have jumped 'the life
to come'). If we heard 'the chimes at midnight',
they didn't warn me when I took a wife.
In different longitudes we learned our plight:
you married, too, but kept your locked heart true
to once upon a time; I lost love's sands
as I turned the glass. But now I see you
clearly, held close to ancient stones. Touched and
charged by signs of times past in my true face,
you watch my hands, frantic to slow Time's race.

7. Stone

The stones that clothe our bedroom have been twice
addressed: first on the hillside, rude and bare;
then by the mason as he shaped and spliced
young granite. He taught it form, face to stare
through the lost years to this husband and wife,
bedded down-warmly in a wintry dawn.
What impulse brought them to a foreign life
and home where each, in love, could be re-born?
Four times a lifetime has this farm survived,
the stones out-staring sunshine, snow and wind:
facing our own storms taught us to revive
the ways we look and love and speak our minds.
If stones wear faces that we all can see,
bear your true face and so give life to me.

8. Slate

This salted field is finger-fenced with slate;
we walk the edge on sea-ground stones in sand.
I ask you if it is my fault or fate
I come to you so late; you draw your hand
through mine like silk and turn me face to face.
No other love can recompense for this:
revealed, we seek from lips and fingers grace
to give and take small gifts of shells, a kiss.
I touch you as we cross a bridge, to shield
you from the burning of our boats; but hold
too hard, like slate posts in a salted field.
Kissing your fingers then just makes me bold:
since stones 'heart' at your finger tips' behest,
move mountains, love, and set my heart at rest.

Epithalamium

The chambers of a climber's heart
are as the caverns of the sea:
void until hard rock plays its part.
Waves, like feelings, wash in to plead

a case, grinding down resistance
in all but the coldest of stones.
Love is just the same: cleaves a glance
of *this, this* beloved; close, alone;

time after time. At Bosigran
huge waves hound their own sound; granite
boulders shudder, split, grind to sand.
Above stalled climbers stand, tied tight

by the radial sweep of air
to the sine curve of wall and slab.
The flashing cliffs give nothing fair
but to the brave and bold - who grab

in mirror-stone for finger holds -
while fearful dance, hands stammering.
Belayed again, moves are retold
with pride, but climbers know the ring

of truth: ropes (like words) whisper falls
from grace are held by trust. What more
is love? These partners burned there, called
out their care; dared to excel; saw

too, how they might tie each other
together with much more than rope.
Rock guides are for any lover.
True marriage is a route of hope

into the flat, 'quick perspective
of the future': secret – unknown
to those who find they cannot live
and love forever. Coldest stones.

But for *this* husband and *this* wife,
filled chambers of their heart will be
tied always to the flashing cliffs,
above the caverns of the sea.

Your Heart's Trees

Trees flourish at your heart's door,
their polished branches shining
in the black-bright Essex rain.

You play their green strings for me
when I come to visit you.
The leaves of their whispered sound

fall upward to my dulled heart,
which is not prepared for them.
Be gracious: I am your guest.

Again and again, because
of you, I'm hurt by beauty –
and grow each time more tender.

The Riddle of Love

There are two men
married to two women.
One man loves one woman;
one woman loves one man;
one woman loves two men;
one man loves two women.

The man who loves one woman
lives with her but doesn't sleep with her.
The woman who loves one man
doesn't live or sleep with him
- she lives alone.
The woman who loves two men
lives with one but doesn't sleep with him;
doesn't live with the other but sleeps with him.
The man who loves two women
doesn't live or sleep with one of them;
doesn't live with the other but sleeps with her
- he lives alone.

The man who loves one woman
cannot live without her.
The woman who loves one man
cannot live with him.
The man who loves two women
cannot live with one of them,
cannot live without the other.
The woman who loves two men
cannot live without either of them.

The men tell their men friends
about these lives and loves.
The women tell their women friends
about their lives and loves.
The friends tell their
husbands and wives
about these lives and loves.
The husbands and wives
tell their men and women friends
about these lives and loves;
but no-one solves the riddle.

Three Haiku

From here:

Stormy parenting,
But, on the rocks, you gave a
Tempest in a book.

The next moment:

Engage brain, you said,
And I did 'till 22.
Trail and error now.

And the next:

Visiting again:
You're not anywhere; I've checked.
I really miss you.

Bryony Noble

The Funerals

After each funeral, and time had ticked off another friend,
we would walk to Whitcliffe and overlook the town.
Up there we stood on the stone outcrop, the rock plateau,
etched with our lichen bound green dreams.
Drunk on emotion and fooled by nostalgia,
we were somehow able to push reality to one side as if it were a bookcase
and as the volumes fell, each page told its own story.

The worm trails gouged into this rock of our roaring youth,
revealed the names of football teams, pop songs and girls.
"Come on you Blues." "We hate West Brom."
"We can't get no satisfaction no no no no no."
"Tim loves Jo" and "Dave loves Gina."
"Touch Tina's titties if you dare!"
Hot thigh frightened we were far too scared.

As these memories were ghosting the wood,
the book case stood upright and straight.
We meandered back to the order of present lives.
And on returning home we would say
"It was sad, sad but it was good, good
to meet people and relive the past,"
when asked about the funeral.

Bill Allison

Sea Palling on the North Norfolk Coast is an important place for the Noble family. After the devastating floods in 1953/4, our father (who was a Civil Engineer working for the Ministry of Agriculture and Fisheries) was dispatched from York - where we lived - to Norfolk. So we all moved to Norwich. Father was responsible for the work to push back the sand dunes and build a concrete sea wall.

I was born in 1951 and as a two year old my earliest memories are of the orange and green bulldozers of a company called May and Gurney working on the Sea Palling gap - a steep access ramp where they could get onto the beach.

Funnily enough, my wife and I happened to be on holiday last year in Norfolk and I made a pilgrimage back to the site where surprisingly little had changed! Photos of the trip show that Sea Palling is not the most attractive seaside place, but it has historically been an access point for fishermen and traders.

In the photo below, you can see the sea wall built after the '53 floods. The plan was that the dunes would cover the wall and be anchored by it. This has largely been achieved, but in places erosion has exposed it. The groynes that were built eventually could not stop the scouring action of the sea. There's another photo that shows me standing with arms outstretched. The ramp is really very steep on both sides. I hadn't remembered that, but then when I was first there the situation was more like the photo of a picture in the local cafe, which shows the devastation.

I have a couple of black and white photos from when we lived in Norfolk - some taken on a day out on a motorboat on the Broads with my grandparents who were both keen photographers.

I think our time in Norfolk had a great impact. I have returned many times - mainly sailing on the Broads but also feeling very at home with the wide open space - so much sky! I love the sound of the water rippling as you sail along with the rustling of the reeds and the fluttering of the "two tone" green leaves of the bankside willow trees.

Tim was right in the poem. I had a plastic and tin toy bulldozer. It had black rubber tracks and looked just like the May and Gurney equipment working on the dunes. I also remember sitting in a cafe at Sea Palling (or what was left of one) on a site visit with father when mother had brought us along. I can clearly remember the sunlight shining through the green glass fishing float globes hanging from the ceiling - so 1950's.

We often used to accompany father on his site visits. At that stage he had acquired a huge old Humber ex-military staff car - the sort that Monty used to have. Tim and I always thought it ran on water as every now and again father would stop the car and borrow our picnic mugs to fill the leaking radiator with ditch water!

We returned at least once after father had been transferred to London, and stayed in a caravan. I remember the wind-blown sand hitting your ankles as you walked on the beach and also how you could quickly hide from the wind in the dunes and find sunshine hollows. But then we weren't supposed to be in the dunes because the marram grass was not meant to be disturbed!

Jeremy Noble

49

Two of Dad's Sonnets

Bryony

Fear was a big factor in my childhood. Despite adoring the scary pictures of witches and creatures, my own mortality plagued me as a girl and still does as an adult. Although it's likely a symptom of uncertainty, one aspect that was never in doubt was Dad's solidarity. He was writing this sonnet while the two of us were on a weekend in Croydon. Lolloping in and out of sea and sand, I kept checking where he was, mostly so I could find my way through holiday makers, back to tea and sandy tartan blankets. I never doubted he wouldn't be still sitting like a rotund Buddha in a mountaineering t-shirt, notepad in hand, because that was where he always was. That and many other holidays by the sea blur in a rush of adrenaline as the wave careers into my legs; it didn't matter that I was supposed to be strong and wasn't sure if I could be, because Dad had my back, literally. There wasn't a wave his big frame couldn't brave: reckless good fun.

Phoebe

Dad was my grumpy rock, but he was never good at apologies. Mostly this was due to the fact that a lot of arguments with his children were to do with his own inner child panicking that we were somehow going to follow his less than brilliant example, that somehow the world would find out that he didn't actually know anything, could do anything. He worried unnecessarily; typical father. A lot of unnecessary pain became inflamed and infected over the years. I remember watching proceedings, flabbergasted that differences in adults could arise from their being so similar (toenails included). Blistering bluster aside, Dad was astute enough to realize that we would be O.K., one way or another, although we weren't so sure, or were pretending to be sure. This is the best Dad could do by way of an apology, a long time coming and well said.

Bryony Noble

Epithalamium

Tim was always a part of our daughter Sally's life. We have a favourite picture of her, aged 12 months, fast asleep whilst belayed to a rock below one of the climbs Tim and I were doing for his book.

Sally had been the president of her university climbing club when she got married, and she and her fiancé were keen and good climbers, so she was delighted when Tim asked if he could write a poem to read at her wedding. He read the poem in the church with great presence and it was a memorable element of the service, especially for the many climbers present.

I love the poem, not just because I think it is a very good one, but because it was written by my friend about a part of life we both cared for deeply.

Poetry is so much more powerful when read by the person for who it is written. This one is very precious to Sally and it hangs on the wall of her house.

Richard Brown

Tim

My own final connection with Tim is indelible. I was with him in the moments of his death and I saw his leaving of our world.

And although time is passing many of us can't stop thinking about him and who can do better than that – to be remembered so much, to be thought of so well?

I first met Tim as Jo's new man in a restaurant in Chelmsford. Bridget and I went in and he was the first thing we saw. First impressions never leave you – he was large, obscuring the chair on which he must have been sitting. He was rotund in a ripe, shiny way. Smartly dressed, if a little old-fashioned. A worldly – wise cherub grown into mature years, somewhat out of time. Beaming brightly.

And his voice – plummy, rich, the voice of a teacher, actor, broadcaster. Polished words, manicured, floated into the air between us. We chatted – he declaimed.

I got to know him better. Unfailingly gracious, clever, puckish. He felt more past than future; but more sense than non-sense. Overcoming some struggles with himself. Getting longing and living in balance, because Jo was the complete compensation for what he had lost.

A big man indeed. Noble.

Terry Turner

Silbury Hill

Seek me:
strip off this skirt of grass
that hides the curves of terrace, spur and ditch,
to find beneath the tiered baulk of chalk
the vast perspective of the years.

Measure me:
mark out, then draw the wattle fence and star
that binds this skin of earth to flinty core.
I was antler-dug, shouldered into air,
my bodying-forth a product of men's fears.

Study me:
how am I tomb of warrior or king?
My pregnant squat and stare
is surely stony symbol of the womb
that year on year conceives and bears.

Speak me:
'Sil' and 'Sol' are metaphors for man.
My annual agony and pride cry out for words
to bring alive the imagery of birth
and show all men the mysteries of The Goddess's tears.

From Cefyn Bryn, by Arthur's Stone

From Cefyn Bryn there is no sign
of Yellow Top or Thurba Head:
these buttresses lie buckled under
millstone grit and harrowed land.
Held tightly in an ancient sine,
they reel and dip beneath the weight
of menhirs high on Cefyn Bryn
that keep the 'home of Arthur' from the light.

But from the shore at Culver Sand
the limestone walls lurch in and out
like palsied warriors who would shrug off
the tyranny of gritstone and mythic grave.
By Kilboidy, East and Western Slad;
down Redgut, Blackhole and Tears Point,
these riddled, pitted limestone walls
breed caves that undermine the settled land.

On Cefyn Bryn ancient gritstone fears
the slow dissolve of myth in time;
tries to hold the land in fee to dreams;
spurns the scientific truth in caves.
For, at Mitchin Hole and Paviland
- hidden in the folds of Gower's coast
- lie bones of mammoth, horse and man,
sheltered by the lime for thirty thousand years.

The Stone Bull

No hunter brought this bull,
snorting, to the deep cave:
he was artist-penned, full
profile, ochred to a wave

of rock. Never cow-licked
by tongues, but drools of lime;
nor trapped by cunning, but tricked
out by design, this prime

beast's held by painted hands.
They have ringed him, humbled
his hooves' tattoo on sand
to a trip and stumble

under old stalactites.
His haunch is volcano:
an eye of malachite
rolls and glares at us. Though

his heart throbs lodes of ore,
rust leaks from crystal veins.
Made before matadors,
he faces endless pain

from stick-men with huge spears.
His bellow is fossil;
but it can't stop the fear
spurt of each spore that will

tether him for ever -
as the priest-artist meant
it to, perhaps. Whatever
lurid tourists invent,

his pigment blood on stone's
more sacrificial myth
than art: animal bones
litter the labyrinth.

Men kill what they revere
most - in manger or stall;
by suffering each year,
this bull holds me in thrall.

A Wave of the Sea

What is that high sound in the air?
Is it the soom of water round the headland,
or the sighing of old sand grains in
the white dunes?

What is that high sound in the air,
hiding the hill's harshness,
drawing taut the note of keening from
the black gull?

It is a wave of the sea,
leaping beyond paradise and wilderness
to its last harbour, life's horizon,
catching from nights of moon
strength to sweep the shores of heaven.

Sailing to Africa

It's not that you are undecided:
there's silver gleaming on the other hand,
and the sea's preened - its best slick self's beside
the soon-to-be-affianced - slopping charm. "Stand

by the rail," he's said, "turn and surprise me."
In profile you smile, almost mean it, too.
Carrying just a small bag, a skirt and tee
shirt? I interpret an impulse that you

hadn't understood. All those watched games he's
played, reading as love your leaks down cold cheeks.
You owe him, don't you, for these gifts - a fee
simple? What could be more natural? "'Seek

for the sword that was broken'; where it dwells
can we? Will this man, married, be as good
as it'll get? Wedded without church bells,
shall we be flat-happy as the sea? Could

I be myself?" The picture shows your fears.
Though the treat, bright Africa's in sight,
I can see the small bag is packed with tears
you still need to weep. Do I know I'm right?

You pincer-grip the rail tight, one hand
bravely backing up the other: the smile's
equivocal as half-glimpsed foreign land.
Besides, I know the dates. You're dreaming miles

round the world, past the camera and the man,
through job, a different husband and a child,
to be lost again in your first passion.
The future seems too balanced with the wild

other gone. Under Himalayan skies
I wake alone from a dream of palm trees,
rings and wasted years. On a hot sea, my
true love sails to Africa without me.

Rain Forest

Above:
    The shrapnel rain burst
    The stab of lightning
    The flying leaf-shards
    The darkened hollows
    The magic carpet
    The bird-filled havens
    The vibrant thrumming
    The steaming greenness
    The forest girders
Between:
    The loom of lightness
    The burgeoning brightness
    The bearded tree trunks
    The mask of tendrils
    The hum of bird song
    The stink of bird life
    The skeet of bird calls
    The web of insects
    The strength of iron wood
Below:
    The barking river
    The tangled rapids
    The oily mud pools
    The fluttering shallows
    The drench of bushes
    The snake's incision
    The sweat of fever
    The slap of stinging
    The fear of drowning
    The rot of clothing
Underneath:
    The thrust of vision
    The glittering mirror
    The gaudy bead gift
    The splendid quest
    The missionary zest
    The desperate burden
    The seeds of doubting
    The native parting
    The faltering heartbeat
    The lunatic trip

Climber

Your eyes float to a patch of red,
splashed against the blue-black
gripstone. You measure distances,
height, movements; await a fall.

His fingers splay in tension,
torquing pebbles near his mouth.
His breath hangs in the balance
on a fulcrum of self. He is centred.

As the flat earth weights you down,
he gives himself entire, fragile as
the clutched crystals, to the axial
spin of stone, the radial sweep of air.

Writing on Rock

All fired up and fueled on memories
of rock, Terry found it for us, five fields
from Overton, down a quiet Gower
slad, above a tetchy and corrosive sea.

It had been rolled there, obviously, left
to rot, its limestone lagging started, its
slab-cladding cracked. This stone boiler
required attention, so we rigged the gear.

No engineer of stone could have predicted
how we'd feel, high on those flakey plates,
mapping the flared cracks with bared hands,
reaching for fault lines and into rusty holes.

We were descaling The Boiler all day, testing
everything we held against other touchstones
in books or self. Ropes thrummed and slackened;
metal rang alarms; anxious calls riveted us.

For hours we carefully mapped the structure
of the cliff, fixing the image, keeping it in mind.
Then we left to write up neat reports on Gower
limestone and the deep tectonics of our fears.

Tuolomne Meadows, California,

is Indian country, where those bright
fires are really dangerous berries
of tall pines, where the stone of moonlight
hones Tressider Peak - not yet buried

in a scalp of stars and Glacier Lake,
by day a clear trinket, mirror-tracks
an old canoe's thin dribble of wake.
These names clog our forked tongues: Piwyack,

Tenaya, Medlicott.Tuolomne
is soft as pipe smoke, aspirated
breath:Twa-lum-knee. Here, Ahwahanee
Indians lost tribal lands to hated

white men; then painful history takes
me hours to read. Until sleep brings relief,
lightning flickers over Mammoth Lakes
and the hot springs boil in disbelief.

Off Tioga Pass, morning mist flies
ragged flags of truce as we start each
climb into a tight red fist of sky
- then wait for shadow-nets to catch

us on the bleached carapace of stone.
Here, rock blisters like skin; quartz,
spills from the wax candle of the dome,
slips from hot fingers. Every thought's

of double-cross. Puffs of cumulus
rise faster than we can above
ourselves, so anger ambushes us
daily in the high country where rough

justice is chief. First, harsh words in tents
(without reservation, pipe of peace),
then livid looks; counting coup; silence.
Who can be braves in council when each

swig of fire-water wine's a bout
between warring friends? By Glacier Lake
we let our friendship cool and snuff out,
and renegade, left the domes to take

different trails out of Indian lands.
But later, lower down, we found
the truth: pride in taking a Last Stand
meant we'd lost the Happy Hunting Ground.

Bow Wall

That day of the fall he knew
it might happen, at the edge
of thought, as he climbed up through
big flakes, unroped, to the ledge

below the bow - though the shock
came much later. Tied in tight,
he stopped talking, let the rock
speak about itself. But light

leached from the hill; long waves, stiff
in the wind, hounded the sound
of their own breaking and the cliff
shuddered. Every hold he found

was cold. Hands stammered then stalled
(granite gives nothing back
but to the brave and bold).
Hauled by himself to the black crack

under the roof, he could see
the steps across the 'pancake'
to the slab, but not how he
could jam his hands or then make

friction into fact. Ropes swung
idly in a damp sea-haze.
"This time," he called down, then hung
from bone, not sinew, and gazed

into mirror-stone. The swing
caught me out; I fed him slack.
Not on jams, but underclings
he launched out and up to smack

the top. Down the vacant air
he fell; grabbed, and turned sideways.
Fear was tattooed to his stare.·
It will stay that way, always.

Dharlang Valley Expedition, 1979

for Nick Pitts-Tucker

Watch the super eight film again. We're led
by your spread fingers: pointing; explaining;
prising the prismatic; stabbing at maps
on Sersank while our flag snaps overhead.
Your best recorded line? The jeep, lurching
to the abyss, scares; but you cut the crap
- nautically: "On the port beam, so to speak!"
Pitched food-light in Dharlang, the porters hold
breath and hearts as you scan the valley,
seeking the secret pass amongst myriad peaks.
We ford the river; then you gently scold
us up a rotting glacier (alley
of fear) to pass and Kingdom of Zanskar.
Point now, and I'll follow you, high or far.

A View to Kanjiroba

for John Tyson

The Langu runs colder by night,
cuts the rune of its passing deep
in bed rock, grinds boulders the height
of houses to sand while we sleep.

Dawn: across a gossamer bridge.
The white river spits, roars applause
at first stage-struck steps to the ridge;
deep icy fears begin to thaw.

Tortoises, with dusty homes high on
raw backs, we climb two thousand
feet, seeing the last village. My
camera jams, full of glacier sand.

At Dalphu, Tyson wrote, he found
'old friends', 'the toughest men' who will
carry long over savage ground.
Our sherpas shepherd us uphill

to this particularity,
this brush of cultures new with old.
But fretting on the quality
of light, my lens is held by bold

and bashful eyes: some tiny girls
carry baskets full of stones
from the gorge. On a word, they hurl
loads, again bend backs and small bones.

Rag-clad, mud-shod, they let the cruel
path re-claim them. Ashamed, incensed,
I want to ferry all Langu's
stone to atone for my presence.

From Dalphu there's a clear view through
to Kanjiroba we'd come six
thousand miles to see - and the hewed,
the hand-made trail, where Tyson fixed

his tree bridges. Do the toughest
men move towards, always towards
the mountain, or find their longest
journeys are the journeys inwards?

The Climber

Where and when is the mountain,
unobserved and without consciousness?
What is this thing?
Steel-hard basalt
Ice-glazed granite
A somnambulance of mist
Silence
Only within his imagination and the reach of his arm does the world exist for
the climber
Upwards
Upwards
Though tied to the misty chasm
Drawing the cord out ever further
What place is this for flesh and bone?

And then, for the briefest of moments, a towering troll goddess emerges
from the vapours
And the mountain crow salutes her three times from the void
Raising his head the climber sees her face
And in so doing endows her with life and aspect
Her eye is steel-hard basalt
Her face is ice-glazed granite
In this short moment she lives through him
Proud
Uncaring
Terrifying
Sublime

Where and when, then, is the mountain,
unobserved and without consciousness?
Only within a fragment of a life
Where self and the world co-create
So may the brave overcome,
The curious discover,
The passionate love,
For in their own times, finite and whole, each has made a world.

Mike Copper

Lifestone

Every man begins his time with a stone
to shape, out of which he carves
the twists and curves and sometimes grander sweeps
that is the substance of his days.

At first surface scratching showing
a boy, learning to cut and mark
trying to find a style of his own
and sometimes stubbing his hand..

Then the freewheeling swirls of a young man,
taking risks and gouging deep.
Now a plateau, smoothed flat, a time for change.
A family cut in the stone.

Blending patterns he becomes a craftsman,
flicking subtlety into the rock.
These are the days of a master mason
building his own cathedral.

And when he dies his actions and glories
remain cut into his lifestone.
Carved as large as his life itself.
He was a man. This is what he did

Every man begins his time with a stone
to shape, out of which he carves
the twists and curves and sometimes grander sweeps
that are the substance of his days

Bill Allison

Tim's poetic muse was stirred by this expedition through the Great Himalayan Range.

Quite right, too. On a scale of 1-10 for adventure, this was about 9. Three high passes, two mighty glaciers, a crumbling ice fall and an awesome river crossing in a box strung 100 feet above the rushing waters.

Four of us went on this journey. Tim and Bill made a brilliant Super 8 film of it. Starting with our rumbling train from Delhi to Pathankot, provisioning in that grubby little railway town, then bus and jeep rides deep into the old princely state of Chamba.

Tim caught well the trio of cliff-track-abyss. We survived nonchalantly and made our way up to the Sach Pass (14,500'). Then down, down into the Chenab Gorge crossed by a box strung on thin cables above the racing green turbulence of that mighty river.

Up, up again with our cheerful porters to cross the Sersank Pass (17,300'), almost vertically, to where our flag snapped in the wind and our porter guide sniffed out the yak dung trail that alone could lead us down and out through the 4,000' icefall into Dharlang.

Dharlang. Unvisited. Uninhabited. At the base of a glacier that leads for many miles to the peaks of Nun and Kun, one of the longest in the Himalayas. Icy cold crossing at dawn.

Icy cold camps on the cracking glacier. Then spot the break in the Great Himalayan Ridge that at 18,752' is the Poat La . A grinding climb over snowfields. A breathless summit. We are in Zanskar.

Our porters cheer. They had never before made their crossing into Little Tibet.

The Super 8 is now a DVD. You can get one from Bill or Roger or Nick*. Thanks, Tim.

Nick Pitts-Tucker

* Bill Blackburne, Roger and Nick Pitts-Tucker

From Bedfordshire To Norway: Tim's Poem 'Climber'

When I was eighteen years old I took part in an expedition to the Jotunheim mountains in Norway organised by the Bedfordshire Schools' Exploration Group, with Tim as one of its leaders. Two landscapes as different as Bedfordshire and the Norwegian mountains would be hard to find and I have been drawn back to such places time and again ever since. Although we took part in many adventures that summer (not many of them compatible with modern ideas of health and safety!) my abiding memories centre on the austerity of the landscape: the black dripping crags; the creaking glacial ice; the silence.

Yet such places have no inherent or essential power. They require us to observe them in order to exist *as* wild and sublime. Unobserved, what is a mountain or a forest? Like the rocks and stones we are part of the world, and it is through us that the world experiences itself.

Tim's poem *Climber* exposes us to a world brought alive by the act of climbing. In the brief moment described, the crag is transformed by the presence of the climber, while the climber exists *as* a climber only because of his interaction with the crag. As the locus of action the rock becomes more than a piece of lifeless geology, it is endowed with character and significance. In such moments we do more than exist in the world, rather the world and the individual create each other.

To live a life of adventure, creativity, passion, curiosity and wonder endows the world with meaning. Tim aspired to live out these values and, as a teacher, to inspire them in others. This is a spirit that will live on through his poetry.

Mike Copper

The last time I climbed with Tim was on what he was describing as his private crag, in France, a small granite outcrop in the woods, high up on the edge of the escarpment running above Tim and Jo's wonderful rural retreat in the Auvergne. That afternoon's outing bore many of the hallmarks of a typical climbing day with Tim. From the outset there was a sense of adventure and uncertainty as to what we would find. (How many days were spent searching for that 'esoteric gem' in a hidden Cornish zawn or a high up Welsh cwm?). Tim had only a well-creased sheet of A4 with a hand drawn basic map and topo, which necessitated multiple attempts forging up tiny roads and tracks, glimpses of rocks through the trees before we finally reached the crag and scrambled down to the bottom. As ever, Tim quickly read the rock, sized up the plum lines, most of which were dressed with a minimum of winking steel bolts, and then sent me to lead up into the unknown. Tim contributed his customary enthusiasm and confidence bolstering shouts.

On that occasion, Tim followed one or two routes but was quite happy to do most of his climbing vicariously, watching me from below, asking for detailed descriptions of a move or a piece of rock, offering support or comment. I loved that about him. He was very good at enjoying your experience, and knowing the thrill and satisfaction you derived from it, without any resentment or frustration that he had not on that occasion been able directly to experience it for himself. A day climbing with Tim was incomplete without a shout of 'full-bore, David!' coming up to you as you heaved and huffed over some sticky overhang or up some troublesome jamming crack. I never did find out the derivation of 'full-bore', but we all knew its meaning. When Giles Atkins and I returned from climbing Le Grand Casse in the Vanoise alps (our first proper Alpine summit), Tim was there to meet us at the bottom, beaming, every bit the proud parent or teacher of us his junior charges. I think he was just happy that we had experienced something of the elation and satisfaction and pure sensual enjoyment that he himself had known and treasured so well from those times in the 'high places' as he would describe them.

I am indebted to Tim for getting me back into climbing, and for creating opportunities for being in the mountains in ways I had assumed would be beyond me. But I am also grateful to him for introducing me to the world of writing about mountains. For several years when Tim and I were both teaching in Wiltshire, a fixed point in the autumn calendar was the Friday night drive north to the Smiths' warm welcome in Sheffield and the Mountaineering Literature Festival at Bretton Hall the following day. Boxed into Tim's ancient VW Golf, with the Penguin Café Orchestra playing on the cassette, windscreen wipers smearing the November drizzle, I remember these journeys with great fondness for the conversation shared. Somehow the dark open road (we would always take the slower Fosse Way through the Cotswolds, rather than the motorway) seemed conducive to exploring these passions we shared. What was the point of mountaineering writing? What did good writing about climbing look like? Why did the climbing magazines print so many join-the-dots accounts of trips and expeditions and so few poems or philosophical reflections on the personal or political significance of climbing and mountains? The next day, these discussions would continue at the festival, often in response to one of the lectures or presentations, which would confirm or contradict our views on the health or otherwise of climbing literature.

Craig Meagidh, Jacks Rake, Gimmer Crag, White Ghyll, Cwm Idwall, Tryfan, Belle Vue Bastion, Zelda, Wintours Leap, Saxon, Gurnards Head, Anvil Corner, Mitre, Chairladder, Les Bans massif des Ecrins, Aiguille de Vanoise, Papillion Ridge. A good number of my most unforgettable days on rock, in the mountains or by the sea, were with Tim. Not every day was a success, in the conventional sense. Several outings ended in dubious abseils off a cracked flake half way up the wrong gully, after hours of searching the rock for any clues as to the right way up. But this was one of the other lessons I hope I have learned from Tim. Succeeding isn't everything. Getting out there is as important as getting to the top. To dream and to dream big is just as important, maybe more important than realising all your dreams.

When Giles and I arrived at the foot of Alpe d'Huez for our first alpine season, Tim produced a hit list of long researched routes that would easily have filled three Alpine seasons. After the long ascent to the hut at the start of the route up Les Bans in the Ecrins, I woke for the always hideous Alpine pre-dawn start to find Tim already outside. Thick cloud hung heavy, obscuring even the start of the climb over the Bergshrund. Waiting until the cloud had lifted to set off meant we were much too late to have a realistic chance of getting to the top, but nevertheless we made our way steadily up the steep crevassed glacier that felt, to my novice eyes and legs, Himalayan in scale. Mid way up, now in gorgeous sunshine, Tim admitted defeat, his dodgy knees calling time, and we headed back down.

I'm pretty sure that had we carried on we would have ended up spending the night on some icy shelf near the summit. I don't mind that we never got anywhere near the top. Being there in that immense field of white and blue snow and ice, Tim's experience and confidence and enthusiasm made safe and accessible this strange and wonderful environment. These moments enriched my life. These moments with Tim shaped my perspective on myself and on the world and on how I wanted to live in the world.

David Trelawny-Ross

Take In Mr. Noble!

There was something devilish about Tim when I first met him. His beard and Reactorlite Aviators were slightly menacing to me as an impressionable youth. He was, for many climbing trips always Mr. Noble, never Tim, which was bizarre because it was often only him and me climbing. It was always a cautious, "Take in Mr Noble," or some other climbing command - until I was 18 when I demanded that I should be allowed to call him Tim. "I never said you couldn't," was the response.

In those early days, I quickly got to know that Tim came with a passion for books, poetry, Bob Dylan and Shakespeare. It was infectious. There was always a trail of books and writing, whether it was his own or other people's, leading to Tim.

Tim always wanted to know your news and what you had been up to. Everything was "Full bore!" He would know in great detail the routes being talked about, whether he had climbed them or not. He organised many climbing trips and often wrote about them. I remember reading his poem of 'Bow Wall'. These trips also created long-lasting connections between different people that Tim brought together.

We also shared other adventures, including a surreal winter's day salmon fishing on the Spey dressed in plastic mountaineering boots, a day at Oban Market watching the selling and buying of highland stock and more notably sailing, where he would unleash a very gifted and competitive side of himself. He let me hold Phoebe when she was a tiny tot and would subject both Phoebe and Briony to trips to Dartmoor to ride our family's horses - Journeyman (whom he called Germanim) and Rummy.

For me there are two Tim words that will always connect me with him: 'apprenticeship' and 'mentor'. Tim generously guided me towards what were the truly classic climbs around the UK, but he also mentored me in other areas of my life and encouraged me to write of my own experiences and review books for the Climbers' Club. Perhaps his last and most important bit of mentoring for me was his advice to read every day to my own daughter from the moment she was born. It's something I've adhered to and often as I pick up a book to read with her, I find myself holding a memory of Tim.

John Baker

I first met Tim around 1988 when Terry Gifford introduced us. Tim was working on his book *Great VS Climbs of the Lake District* and Terry had suggested I could be involved as a climbing photographer. I enthusiastically embraced this idea as it would give me the chance to get to know the Lake District better and I liked the concept of the book. We visited a variety of locations and climbed with a number of different climber/models, in such places as Langdale, Borrowdale, Dow Crag and most memorably, Eskdale. The Eskdale trip was a big day out with the long walk up to Esk Buttress and, for me, an ascent of *Medusa* with Tim and Renny Croft which enabled me to get my favourite photo from the project, of Renny on the top pitch.

Following this ascent, we continued up to the East Buttress of Scafell for Tim and Renny to climb *Mickledore Grooves* with me photographing from the ground with a long lens. We then had to return down Eskdale to the camp site at Boot, only just making last orders in the pub and finishing the day by eating cold pizza (home-made by Renny's wife) in the moonlight.

At this time, I was working as the Deputy Editor of *High* magazine and Tim became a frequent contributor, offering articles about other climbing trips and we were always happy to accept his submissions and we continued to work together as Tim became one of our pool of book reviewers.

Tim and I continued to climb together occasionally and meet up in the Lake District every so often. He would spend a holiday every year at Low Bridge End Farm below the Castle Rock of Triermain and we would join Tim, Sally, Phoebe and Bryony for a weekend, us camping in the farmer's field.

The next big climbing trip I made with Tim was to the Alps where we were due to stay at one of the campsites in Bourg D'Oisans and climb in the Ecrins. The primary target was the Aiguille Dibona, a beautiful pyramidal spike of a mountain. Due to my work commitments the rest of the group were able to get out there sooner than us and we arrived on a Sunday only to be told that we were heading for the Dibona the following day. My protestations were to no avail as I was firmly told the forecast was good and the beds in the hut were booked.

The walk-in to the hut proved to be as tough as I expected as I had had no acclimatization or preparation, unlike the others, and I arrived a long way behind them and suffering, and to add to the mix my asthma was responding badly. I headed straight to bed, though did get up briefly to force down some soup, and to warn Tim that I might not be able to be his climbing partner the following day. However, the recuperative power of sleep worked and I felt able to start the next day and am so glad I did as we had a fantastic time.

We climbed mostly the Madier Route, around 20 pitches, and on the first section to the Boell Ledges we shared leads. Tim led one of the hard 5a pitches (a big step around and over an overhang) and I took the other hard pitch (a jamming crack). At the Boell Ledges we looked up to see Giles and DTR, who informed us that all the *in-situ* gear had been stripped from the

Fissure Madier and it had become a quite tough, sustained 5b jamming pitch. Discretion took over and we opted for the easier variation of a very nice, long V Diff pitch up a groove followed by a Hard Severe traverse back to the top of the Fissure Madier to rejoin the route. The summit was a proper pointed one with room for only one to sit and be photographed, followed by an abseil and a tricky descent of a snowfield back to the hut. Collecting rucksacks that had been left behind we headed back down to the road and, eventually, the campsite, exhausted but very happy after a magnificent day in the mountains.

When Tim got the house in France with Joanna we were, of course, very keen to visit and on one of our touring camping trips around France we arranged to do so. Tim had sent a hand-drawn map, very pretty but not necessarily practical or to scale. We found ourselves driving up through the forest as night was falling and as one of Tim's crucial directions was to 'turn left at the lighting-blasted tree' we suspected we could be in for a tricky time as it was too dark to pick out individual trees. We continued, getting more and more confused, until the road ran out forcing us to turn around. Luckily we could get a signal on our mobile phone and, risking high roaming charges, we rang Tim and had to try and explain where we were in the forest in order for him to direct us to the house. It worked, and we were soon sharing a glass and laughing about it.

I saw Tim less and less though we did try to keep in touch and we made another visit to the house in France. He would stay with us when events such as the Mountain Literature Festival brought him north. I would often get phone calls from him when he was waiting on station platforms and I still miss answering the phone to hear: "Ah, Lord Smith, what news?"

Ian Smith

"TO REST IS NOT TO CONQUER"

(Selections from Tim's prose writing)

79

Where Men And Moorland Meet

A story about a "town boy" on a Dales farm near Ilkley, told by Tim Noble

Wind-wuthered grit stone walls mark out the boundaries of the farms. The horizon, flexing slowly in the bracken-shimmer, lies no more than three fingers deep in distance from my feet, but sweeps for miles around the fields that stretch to every compass point I turn. I stand in the hayfield of Westmoor Farm, three miles north and east of Ilkley in the Yorkshire Dales, in high June, and look upon the place I lived some thirteen years ago and upon its landmarks and its limits in the folded bowl of moor.

To the north and the west, the double summit of Beamsley Beacon is a watershed. Beyond, and out of sight, is Blubberhouses, and round the Beacon slope lies Langbar dropping to the road. The dipping contours straight ahead run down to Middleton hamlet, and far across the valley of the Wharfe the last of the sun catches the Cow and Calf where I climbed and climbed. These names have meaning only in relation to the moors that give them form: there are other names to know as well.

I turn and wander down the loning that falls from Hungry Hill where all the farm's water springs and collects. It is planted now with young, well-supported trees. Their frost-fingered leaves flash grey then green, twirling in warmer wind that heralds approaching rain.

I'd come back to do a weekend's work on the land. Those years ago I'd rented the farm cottage and taught the sons and daughters of the town from literary texts about the ways of words and world - but learned more of the verities of life and death and the economics of the struggle to survive from harsh walks round the farm's rim on wild nights at lambing time, among long-suffering sheep.

My landlord, Joe Paisley, and his wife Paula taught me then about the land and what it will support: thirteen years of teaching had almost helped me to forget. Such knowledge though, sticks deep, and as I turn into the yard and close the gate, I feel proud I can recall the names of places, skills and things I'd learnt for homework with my hands. The rain starts fitfully as I scrape open the door. The ewes in the barn are moving over straw.

That day had started early in the mist. Behind the farm, though, damp sheep were drying in the breeze. As we walked into the fields, Joe told me how, despite the gales and steady rain throughout the year, they'd managed to keep 700 lambs - and most of them twins. The sky cleared then clouded over. I saw the stunted grass in the hay fields and realised how snow in April holds back growth. In the small barn, sacks of fertiliser were stacked like little houses.

By the time we'd crossed the reservoir, cloud was scrubbing clean the land and moving over fast and grey.

Curlew piped and drummed the air as we moved round the gunrange field and the beck that feeds the eastern arm of the reservoir. In the end-of-the-world field we were at the edge of cultivated land and looked out over bracken and stone to the shooting butts that marched away towards Beamsley ridge. We were going out and into a corner of the walls to clear some stone and level out the ground. In winter the Paisley family have to carry hay some 60 yards uphill into a snow-packed barrier of wall. We were going to build wind-breaks.

In the middle of the wasteland, three tractors stood mute, their rusty, trusty metal radiator grins an earnest of their powers of service all the day. And all the day young Robin Paisley on the power arm and Joe and I with mastiff bucket, harrow and hand sought to bring the waste land within the compass of the farm. All day the sweet but acrid tang of acid gritstone peat caught in our throats. All day I waded ankle-deep in loam, my head awash with smells, hearing only the "whoorp" of moor birds and the muted cough and mutter of the tractors down the wind.

Some of the stones we pulled out of the ground were as big as coffins; they left black gaping wounds across the fleshy peat. Grey they were, wind-scoured above the ground - but acid bleached to dead-bone white below. Some looked like broken megaliths or dolmen-capping lintels brought out of the dark and secret places into light. There was a life in them, rolling or not rolling.

Sometimes they sprang at me or slyly squeezed my fingers against steel as I pushed and heaved to get them into their proper places in the new way of things being built; and sometimes they refused to move and lay uncleft and pagan-firm, wedged deep like faithful thegns around a fallen lord, never to be moved until the earth itself shall fall away. We left them then, buried in unharrowed ground, and drove around them with respect.

The day passed over us unhurriedly - though the wind blew steadily from the north. We carried, dumped and built the stone bases for the wind-breaks in the centre of the block. Three feet of height in a wall gives three square yards of calm down the lee for hard-pressed sheep harried by a north-west blizzard and every ton of stone gives a cubic yard of wall.

Some of the stones we raised could not have been carried by a horse and cart: even the Fordson Major sometimes reared up in alarm, surprised by an evil weight, and had to be counter-balanced by me clinging to its nose and stack. Our wall foundations in parts were only one stone thick: they looked as if they'd grown there, like some forbidden fruit of moorland, sickly-white and strong.

At midday and at three we stopped for sandwiches, cheese and cake and tea. In the lee of our new wind-break, ewe high, we lay and let the blood beat back into our hands and talked about the Test. At half past five, Joe sent me home before I fell into a hole with fatigue. The tractors and the man and son ticked on another hour. I looked back at them from the ridge of the goose field and saw the machines nodding slowly up and down the bumps, still patient at their task. As I watched, the mastiff arm picked up a stone and waved a stiff good night.

The cloud had slowed by the time I could see the farm again. All down the valley of the Wharfe to Otley and beyond, the light was breaking in bright bursts from a riven sky. I walked tiredly around the place I'd put the tractor into years ago, ten minutes after Joe had left me alone for the first time with the reed cutter. He'd had to come and tow me out. The land drains in the lambing field had made the turf as springy as a putting green. Down the final slopes I tried to spot the gimmers, shearlings and lambs and give a name to the ground I'd helped to clear. The heat from the last wall below the gate was ebbing fast as I leant against it in the dusk and looked back at the moor. The far country - there was a name for that field, where I'd been "far out all my [day], and not waving but drowning".

There is a very narrow band of land between the sky and where you stand. It's a trick of perspective, the eyes' deceit that seems to bring the moor close to your feet. But I knew then, as I'd known before and will again that moors behind the farms go on forever and that it takes a life of learning, walking, working in the fields that have been named and claimed before you come to terms with that thin band where men and moorlands meet.

The rain started fitfully as I scraped open the door. The ewes in the barn were moving over straw.

The Dalesman, June 1988

There were seven of us, crawling up the Allt A'Mhuilinn into a big wind with our eyes ice-gummed and beards tinkling. Huge tongues of super-cooled Siberian air were licking tons of spindrift off the crenellated summit plateau of the Ben. The gullies were raging torrents. For a week we had been arguing about gullies and buttresses. Some of us had had quick wins over No. 6 and Crowberry in banked out conditions, while the others had had real contests with the North Buttress and Deep Cut Chimney. So today we were topping the bill on the biggest hill in a decider - and we'd agreed we'd all be on the rocks.

At the hut, Sam the bacon man turned round and swept back down. Big Dave took retching Richard off to walk up Tower Ridge. Richard had done half a dozen routes and left most of his lungs behind to prove it. Bottles of beer and antibiotics had failed to slow him down, and Dave reckoned they could easily go the distance in the time. The rest of us tied ourselves together in deep powder below Observatory Ridge.

As John swam off uphill, my money was on the hill to win on short odds - and well within the hour. But we kept wading in and rolling with the rocks until it was my turn in the ring for pitch two. I remembered it from an easier summer scrap: a smooth slab, cut by a rising two inch ledge. I made two steps and balanced up above a peg. The only rhythm I'd got was a trochaic tattoo of Terror picks on the plate glass slab above. One notch of one axe bit. I arm-locked the wrist sling and slowly mantleshelfed the ledge.

John told me later that he'd been tightening his chin strap and chatting to Lathan when the single nine millimetre started screaming around his kagoule. Snatching at it, he'd been body slammed into the belay peg and pinned in a full nelson until I was counted out and got back on the hill thirty feet below.

I pulled the tag rope in and pointed John at the place where my pick had pulled a plate away. First round to the hill: one fall and one submission. John had a ruminative suck on his asthma inhaler and edged across the ledge, ninety per cent of his banana picks out of the ice. He also found the nerve to grin at the camera. I knew then that the odds had lengthened. The mixed-aged, mixed-weight team from Wiltshire were going to be a match for the mixed ground. But I still had to prove that I could hold my own, so pitch three up the left edge overlooking Zero was mine.

On steep water-ice in a little leftward-leaning groove, I tried every trick in the book to get some relief from the nervous pounding. Without a referee watching, I even tried a long sling over an icy block as a runner, but it shrugged it off. A six inch screw bottomed after two inches and then I heard someone whimpering. I closed my mouth and bridged the groove, crossed a rib and into a cave and in five minutes, I was leaning on a Friend and the ropes and watching John thrash the groove into submission. Round two to us; things were warming up.

John boosted his steroid level on the inhaler and stormed back into a bear hug with an icy bulge. Short powdery traverses - with strenuous sections in between - this was the pattern of the route; and when I'd got out of the awkward bulge at the end of the next traverse, I could have done with a suck on John's steroid stick myself. You didn't need an axe for twenty feet, just frozen mitts on frosted flakes that drooped and overhung. John looked pensive when I flopped down beside him: the inhaler had run out.

Lathan and R.B. had slowed down fast behind us - which was just as well: I didn't want an audience watching me grovelling up pitch five. But John was fully stoked up on Mars by now and ravings about the rocks, so I turned him loose on the steep corner above. It was after lunch and getting cold. Cloud was coming on and my moustache grew icicles. John waded up a trough and over blocks and started jamming up the corner. At forty feet he stopped and started breathing hard. We didn't have another steroid stick. I saw him plant a pick into the right wall. He did an appalling splits and looked back down at his trainer for approval. Talk about playing to the crowd. I thought he was faking it until he called for slack. Now John only does this when he's going to jump. Up or down, it doesn't matter, just so long as he's got enough rope to reach the point that he's chosen. Time for our new winter call of support, and paid out three feet through frozen dachsteins.

'Glow for it! Glow for it!' I shouted through the cloud, and he somersaulted out of sight. I needed a sling for aid to do the same, but I don't think he saw me.

So there we were, four rounds up, with three lovely pitches up the arete in front of us. As we wandered on, we heard paroxysms of coughing from Tower Ridge and stopped to watch and wave as retching Richard came into sight, bent double, marking out the route for the next party.

I wondered if we'd done the crux - the guide and Cold Climbs ignore specifics like that - and in the summer everything was Diff. But then it caught us up and the wind increased as well. With an awful nut low and to his right John had to pull up from the ramp we had followed on the right edge overlooking Point Five, swing across an icy wall using a letterbox and one axe into a slim, loose groove on the left. It looked a stopper for fifty minutes. Following at full stretch, feet splayed wildly on silly bits of ice, I nearly threw in the towel, and up. I was almost beaten. So, rewarding John with my last Mars bar (a cunning ploy to keep him in the lead), and scoffing coffee and sardines in a little niche, I waited to see if Lathan could beat that move.

Half an hour passed. No noise below. John started repeating all my mountain slogans to get me climbing again.

"To rest is not to conquer," he said primly, so I plodded off along the ridge.

It was while he was solving the last little groove below the junction with Zero that I heard the shouting. Looking down the three hundred feet we'd climbed from the sardine niche, I saw Lathan clinging to the crack above the crux. He was waving his axes in the air and hacking at the wall to the right of where he should have been. Now I knew he couldn't climb grade six, and sure enough, as I watched him, he gave a wonderful wail and vanished. A purple flash and a clatter told another tale. His brand new Cassin axe had gone as well. No doubt some scavenging Scot will find it in the spring.

Things looked bad. Two falls and one submission. Was there another of the latter still to come? Lathan was unhurt (impossible) . He wanted to go down with his one remaining axe (almost impossible). He tried the crux again - the proper way this time (impossible). We wasted an hour calling and watching. The night crept over Nevis and we froze. Then R.B. had a go and lead the wall in seconds - his first crux of the holiday. I was aghast. Did my Greater Ranges experience count for nothing then? Now R.B. runs a lot and plays badminton. He also weighs less than one of my axes. Perhaps that's the way to beat a Nevis crux?

"You don't beat the mountain, you beat yourself," John giggled out of the gloom. I tried to thwack him with an adze, but slipped off the stance. Of course, we'd lost the bout. Two falls and two submissions between the teams and more time than the rules allowed. Even the last five pitches up Zero took hours without a deadman. Driving axes, dodging ice chips, hiding from the wind; we made the summit in a black out and waited yet again.

From the freeze box that's the shelter, I shone a headtorch back along the bearing as a beacon. John sat and suffered chocolate and inhaler withdrawal symptoms and got catatonic in the cold. It was nine p.m. We knew that they were wise virgins with full sacks and lights, so we left them to a night on the hill. But as we slunk off down the shoulder of Carn Dearg, the wind hooted and threw ice blocks at us. There was no applause either from Sam or Dave or retching Richard when we got back home at twelve. John had frost nip in a finger and I'd broken a tooth. At three, however, the others shivered in and we all went to bed tired and emotional.

Standing under the cliffs of Stob Coire Nan Lochan two days later, John declared to R.B. and me: "I don't know about you chaps, but I'm a buttress-man myself."

We ran away into the comfort of SC gully and left him gazing at the rocks.

March 1986

No matter where you drive in Nord Pas De Calais, it is impossible to put out of mind the opening words of L.P. Hartley's novel of Edwardian decline, *The Go Between*: 'The past is another country... ' This is because much of the countryside is, quite literally, devoted to other countries.

The cemeteries of allied dead from the First World War are to be found everywhere: sometimes in remote fields, sometimes in the heart of quiet villages and sometimes in the centre of busy thriving towns. American, Australian, British, Canadian, New Zealanders, Indian – even far eastern auxiliaries (China sent 200,000 labourers to support the allied cause and France shipped out some 100,000 Vietnamese peasants and artisans) lie enfolded in French soil.

Indeed, the Canadians have their own tranche of Canada at Vimy Ridge - ground given by the French nation in grateful recognition of the crucial, desperate battle fought in early 1917.

But the past is very much alive here, for the department is a minefield of culture, human stories and historical interest, brilliantly developed by the regional government supported by a superb infrastructure. This is a model of how to regenerate an old mining region - to the lasting benefit of local life – responding to, and mobilizing, the growing worldwide interest in the First World War and family trees. With over five million soldiers killed, countless numbers of people have an ancestor buried somewhere in northern France, or with a name incised on a monument: sooner or later, their descendants will want to discover just where.

The ancient and beautiful capital of Artois, Arras, just twenty minutes from Vimy Ridge, is the perfect base to explore the region; it inspired my wife and me recently to a personal quest. Drawn initially by the lure of the Christmas market and the stunning revelation of the underground stone corridors of the recently-renovated Wellington Quarry, where 24,000 men lived for two weeks before the battle of Arras, we based ourselves for a night in one of the town's many excellent hotels just streets away from the Grand Place. We revelled in the festive atmosphere, sampling the delights of both the market and the best pizzas either of us can remember eating. But our energies were focused on a different target.

As a retired teacher of English, married to an ardent historian of The First World War, the challenge for us both was clear: we were fired up to find and contemplate the graves of two of England's greatest poets, killed only kilometres from each other, a little distance from Arras. As with many of the dead of The Great War, the poets are buried close to where they fell. It is thus possible, within reason, to visit or view both sites.

Wilfred Owen and Edward Thomas are now recognized the world over as seminal influences on the development of English poetry. Owen, whose subject was 'War and the pity of War', produced a handful of poems in half-rhymes, considered to be definitive of the experience of battle. Edward Thomas, writing about the natural world and country life in the rhythms of everyday speech, was given the accolade 'The father of us all' by the late poet laureate, Ted Hughes.

The poets may have met in an Essex training camp where Thomas quite probably instructed the younger Owen in map-reading skills. If only they had conversed at length about their shared passion for writing, however: what then for the future nature and direction of English poetry? Owen was outside the professional literary life of the full time reviewer, but would no doubt have responded to friendly and avuncular advice. Thomas, in his turn, would surely have been moved by the younger poet's intelligence and sensitivity. Independently, they already shared the friendship and patronage of other leading poets and the support of several formidable women: Siegfried Sassoon inspired Owen to write great poetry; his mother, Susan, was the focus of many of his letters from the front. Thomas was the dear friend of America' s soon-to-become most popular poet, Robert Frost; and Helen Thomas, his wife, and Eleanor Farjeon, the author, both adored him.

The timing of our 'expedition' seemed apposite: in London, a play about Edward Thomas, *The Dark Earth and the Light Sky* has attracted big audiences (drawing on the Costa Book Award winner of 2011, *Now All Roads Lead to France, The Last Years of Edward Thomas)*; and in 2014, the centenary of The First World War kicks in. Since our hotel was already taking bookings for these latter celebrations, we thought it best to visit now.

Unusually, Wilfred Owen is buried in a local rather than military cemetery. The village of Ors, straddling the Sambre-Oise canal, is in a direct line from Arras, through Cambrai. The cemeteries are barely noticed by the locals, now, so twice missing the ubiquitous green signs of *The Commonwealth War Graves Commission* and asking directions at both our intended destinations drew a blank; but this, we felt, was curiously reassuring. Walking up past florid decorations of village memorials to the stark and discreet fifty four gravestones of the Lancashire Fusiliers and 2nd Manchesters, who all fell together trying to bridge the Sambre Canal on the morning of the 4th November, 1918, we appreciated the juxtaposition of ordinariness with universality: both graves are overlooked by domestic gardens and sitting room picture windows. The back row of the cemetery contains his grave. Our eyes were drawn to a headstone with a wreath against it: it warmed my heart that Queen Elizabeth's School, Penrith had journeyed here to honour him before us. There were more wreaths at the Cross of Sacrifice – most of them for Owen.

It is a recurring feature of the battlefield graveyards that the great are interred with the good – men and officers together – and the stories of Owen's comrades are as moving as his own. So, LIEUTENANT W.E.S.OWEN M.C. is buried between two privates; and in the same row can be found SECOND LIEUT. JAMES KIRK V.C. who paddled out into the middle of the canal with a Lewis gun to face down the Germans no more than fifteen metres away, while covering the building of a floating bridge. LIEUTENANT COLONEL JAMES NEVILLE MARSHALL V.C., M.C. AND BAR also lies hereabouts. His drive to complete the crossing under a hail of fire led him to take appalling risks (he'd already received and recovered from ten wounds), before he fell with his eleventh and last on the far bank of the canal.

According to Jon Stallworthy's biography of Owen, 'Through this hurricane the small figure of Wilfred Owen walked backwards and forwards between his men, patting them on the shoulder... He was at the water's edge, giving a hand with some duckboards, when he was hit and killed.' If you look over the cemetery hedge above his grave, it's possible to see the point, a thousand yards north from the centre of Ors, where all these men died in vain a week before war end. One may also walk there, along the canal towpath.

According to Thomas's commanding officer, he is 'buried in a little military cemetery a few hundred yards from the battery.' Now, you would suppose that the military cemetery of Agny would be in the village of that name; but it isn't: it's on a little left turn off the Achicourt to Wailly road, three kilometers or so south of Arras. We read the register and found the grave of Philip Edward Thomas close to the entrance. His friend, Robert Frost, wrote to Helen in condolence, 'I want to tell him...that he is a poet.' Just that last word in all its simplicity and import is inscribed at the foot of his headstone.

Edward Thomas was killed on the first day of the Battle of Arras, 1917. An artillery spotter for 244 Siege Battery, he was just emerging from his dugout when the wind from a passing shell simply stopped his heart. He fell without a mark on him. Earlier, he had been reading Shakespeare's sonnets and recorded in his diary, 'Beautiful was Arras yesterday...seeing Town Hall ruin white in sun like a thick smoke beginning to curl.' Right up until that last morning he was observing animals and relishing the local chalk landscape that reminded him so much of his habitual walking paths.

This walking through the old pathways is what has inspired award-winning author Robert Macfarlane in his recent book *The Old Ways: A Journey On Foot* (Hamish Hamilton, 2012), for 'Thomas knew that paths run through people as surely as they run through places, and his poems are filled with images of tracks, crossroads, stiles, fingerposts and waymarkers of many kinds.'

As we followed the small roads back to Calais, thinking of the inhuman circumstances in which these two great poets fought and died, I recalled *The Go Between*: 'The past is (indeed) another country', because, 'they (did) things differently there.' With all their comrades, long may they be remembered and their graves revisited.

More About Ben Nevis

The Allt A'Mhuilinn is the long and remorseless uphill approach to the climbs on Ben Nevis. To fit in a long climb in February, it is necessary to be on the walk-in well before dawn using head torches.

Latham and I, being Ben Nevis novices, followed Tim and John up the climb which, in the conditions, was a serious undertaking. For us, it was a very long, often anxious, but eventually rewarding day, starting the climb at 10.00am and finally getting back to base at 2.00am the following morning.

After Lathan's fall we were very slow and fell steadily behind. Well after dark, Tim and John waited for us on at the small summit emergency shelter but understandably decided that due to the cold, the best course of action was to head down. Tim drove John back to the caravan where we were staying and returned to the Ben Nevis car park to wait for us should we decide against a bivouac on the climb and make it down.

Meanwhile Lathan and I were making very slow, careful progress up the climb, hampered by Lathan's loss of an axe when he fell. Fortunately it was clear and moonlit. Towards the top however, we moved into cloud and when we eventually made it to the plateaux at midnight, we were faced with a white-out. We took a bearing and arrived at the refuge, a small, corrugated iron construction which provided shelter from the wind but was effectively a deep freeze. We sat there for an hour or so, but getting seriously cold, we decided to risk heading down. We took another bearing and set out only to find that after descending a few hundred feet, we dropped out of the cloud into a beautiful, starlit night. With a massive sense of relief and a growing sense of achievement, we headed down and were mightily relieved to find Tim waiting for us with a hot drink.

Richard Brown

The Graves Of The Poets*

Was that the pilgrimage? French fields unfolding?
You had set out to find truth in the landscape
wondering what to read where, from the furrows.
Pages of farm tracks traced hedge and ditch secrets,

deep and beguiling, like Wilfred and Edward;
copses and thickets remembered their whispers.
Did you encounter them, lost in the winter's
hundred-odd headstones?

                    They stand there, like mountains,

calling, conscripting from far beyond England,
larger than home and its everyday archives,
work, and the hard drive of memories and re-drafts.

Tim, we are with you, an army of writers,
marshalled by what you wrote, true to each insight,
guiding us, then and now, back from the trenches.

Will Daunt

* The title of a poem that Tim's notes indicate he intended to write, following the visit
with Joanna to the cemeteries where Wilfred Owen and Edward Thomas are buried.
The account of the visit to the poets' graves (included here) was discovered after this
poem had been written.
'At Takstang Monastery' and 'Where Men And Moorland Meet' are similarly lost
poems, as Tim envisaged the project in October 2014.

Bill Allison

Bill Allison lives in the North of England with his wife and two daughters. He has been retired ten years. However his daughters always say he has not retired but has been regenerated à la Dr Who.

John Baker

John started climbing with Tim in 1982 and they kept in touch (as men do i.e. 'frequently and sporadically', but always with much loyalty) throughout the rest of Tim's life. They spent their time together researching, climbing and writing about many classic routes; it was a symbiotic relationship - Tim knew the routes to do and John was able and willing. All of John's family knew and loved Tim. John is a Public Rights of Way Officer for his local County Council. In his spare time he is a Professional Mountaineering Instructor guiding clients up many of the climbs he first did with Tim.

Richard Brown

I first met Tim when we taught in Wiltshire schools: he in secondary English and me in primary. We met because of our shared interests in teaching and the outdoors, firstly on a writing course, when Tim described a group he organised called Wiltshire Hillcraft Association which ran outdoor pursuits courses for teachers. I decided to attend some of their meets, following a mountaineering course in the Alps. Typically, Tim soon had me signed up for his planned spring half-term Scottish ice climbing trip, the start of many and a long friendship.

Back then Tim lived in Trowbridge, only a few miles from me so the friendship soon developed to include our families and we spent several holidays together in the southern Alps. Tim also introduced me to a local group of rock climbers and later sponsored me in joining the Climbers' Club. We made good use of the club's huts to continue winter and summer climbing.

We also maintained contact through education. Tim moved to Greendown School in Swindon where he was responsible for primary-secondary liaison, and I became head of a Trowbridge primary school. Tim put his passion for Shakespeare to good use by supporting primary schools producing Shakespeare plays and he inspired me and my staff to attempt a tremendously successful production of *The Tempest*. Later, I ended my career in schools and moved into advisory work and small scale farming. Typically, Tim was fascinated by the farming process and visited regularly, one year joining in with the hay making. There were few things Tim was not interested in and knowledgeable about and I was lucky to have his interest and support in so many aspects of my life.

Will Daunt
Between 1985 and 1989, Tim was Will's Head of English in Salisbury. Then Will moved to Lancashire, and the Little and Large of Westwood St. Thomas' English Department kept in touch, largely by Tim's better organized and more persuasive use of the telephone.
Will's sixth poetry collection was published by Lapwing in Belfast in 2013. Any suggestion of other forays into creative writing are purely fictional.

Jeremy Noble
Right up until we both left home Tim and I were always known collectively as "The Boys", probably because we were close together in age and five years older than our younger brother. Tim's teenage years were difficult. Probably no more than any teenager growing up in the 1960's and 70's and during that time our pursuits and interests went in different directions . Tim to the Mountains and I to the Sea. The Mountains and Poetry were always special to Tim and both were intertwined. In later years we rediscovered that childhood closeness and his early death leaves a space where we would have both told each other tales, swapped experiences and listened to his poetry

Nick Pitts-Tucker
I met Tim through his brother Jerry. I was looking for a fourth member for our daring Himalayan crossing over three ever higher passes and the super remote Dharlang Valley. We had plenty of adventures on that trip and Tim made (with Bill) a brilliant 40 minute movie on his Super 8 camera. Friendship ever since. Not surprising!

Ian Smith
Ian has worked for 37 years as a volunteer producing climbers' guidebooks for both the British Mountaineering Council and The Climbers' Club and was presented with the George Band Award 'For Exceptional Voluntary Contribution to Mountaineering' by the British Mountaineering Council in 2017. He also wrote the first ever climbers' guidebook to Jersey (Channel Islands) for the commercial publisher, Cordee. Professionally, Ian has worked as Deputy Editor on three UK climbing magazines: *High, Climb* and *Climber* over 25 years and has had his climbing photographs published in other British and international magazines, books and Journals. He has also proofread and edited numerous books on climbing including writing and illustrating a climbing instructional book for dyslexic children. He was the Journal Editor for The Climbers' Club 1987-91 (as was Tim later) and was Judge and Chair of Judges (2009-10) for the Boardman Tasker Award for Mountain Literature (as was Tim).

David Trelawny-Ross
David Trelawny-Ross was a teacher and later Head of English at comprehensive schools in Swindon, Wiltshire and Sheffield until his life was detoured by illness fifteen years ago. It was in Wiltshire that he got to know Tim. He has been a sometime author, jazz pianist and rock climber. Currently he is committed to enjoying the small things. He enjoys sharing

his house with interesting foreign students and his cat, Charlie. You can hear his most recent music by searching for "david trelawny ross" on Bandcamp or Soundcloud, and you can find his book 'A dream of white horses' on lulu.com.